Poultney Bigelow, Frederic Remington

**The Borderland of Czar and Kaiser**

Vol. 1

Poultney Bigelow, Frederic Remington

**The Borderland of Czar and Kaiser**
*Vol. 1*

ISBN/EAN: 9783337350826

Printed in Europe, USA, Canada, Australia, Japan

Cover: Foto ©ninafisch / pixelio.de

More available books at **www.hansebooks.com**

# THE BORDERLAND
## OF
# Czar and Kaiser

NOTES FROM BOTH SIDES OF

## The Russian Frontier

BY

POULTNEY BIGELOW

ILLUSTRATED BY FREDERIC REMINGTON

NEW YORK

HARPER & BROTHERS PUBLISHERS

1895

Copyright, 1894, by HARPER & BROTHERS.

*All rights reserved.*

TO

# GEORGE KENNAN

*My dear Kennan,—You have travelled Siberia at the risk of your life, and published the truth without malice.*
*This dedication is for the benefit of the few who still question your statements. I tried to do so once, and became,     Your sincere friend,*

POULTNEY BIGELOW

Chelsea Embaukment, London

# ILLUSTRATIONS

| | PAGE |
|---|---|
| GERMAN CUIRASSIERS . | *Frontispiece* |
| RUSSIAN INFANTRYMAN . . . . . . . . | 1 |
| ADVANCE OF RUSSIAN INFANTRY . . . | 5 |
| A BOLD DRAGOON . . . . . . . . | 9 |
| "DRAGOONS, MOUNT !" . . . . . . . . | 13 |
| ONE OF THE CZAR'S BODY-GUARD . . . . . . . | 17 |
| SHOEING COSSACK HORSES . . . . . . . . . . | 21 |
| COSSACKS SCOUTING . . . . . . . . . . . | 25 |
| THE SOLDIER'S SONG . . . . . . . . . . . | 29 |
| A HAIR-CUT IN A CAVALRY-STABLE . . . . . . . . | 33 |
| KUBAN COSSACK, IMPERIAL GUARD CORPS . . . . . . | 37 |
| THE RUSSIAN MILITARY GENDARME . . . . . . . . | 41 |
| ONE OF THE CZAR'S PIRATES . . . . . . . . . | 45 |
| THE THIRD SECTION AT WORK . . . . . . . . . | 51 |
| "I THOUGHT I HEARD YOU SAY, 'COME IN!'" . . . . | 57 |
| IN THE CAFÉ TOMBOFF . . . . . . . . . . . . | 61 |
| A GENDARME IN WARSAW . . . . . . . . . . . | 67 |
| SCENE IN A POLISH VILLAGE . . . . . . . , . . | 73 |
| GENDARME, ST. PETERSBURG . . . . . . . . . | 81 |
| "TWO OFFICERS ARE WATCHING YOU" . . . . . . | 87 |
| A PAGE OF SKETCHES MADE ON THE NIEMEN . . . . | 91 |
| THE FRONTIER GUARD AND THE CUSTOM-HOUSE . . . | 95 |
| A RUSSIAN JEW . . . . . . . . . . . . . . | 98 |
| JEWS AT A PEASANT MARKET . . . . . . . . . | 105 |
| SMUGGLERS ON THE FRONTIER . . . . . . . . . | 111 |
| JEWISH SMUGGLERS AND REFUGEES IN THE HANDS OF THE DRAGOONS . . . . . . . . . . . . . | 119 |

## ILLUSTRATIONS

|  | PAGE |
|---|---|
| JEWISH RECRUITS | 125 |
| CAPTAIN ZINNOWITZ | 131 |
| DRAGOON OFFICER IN STREET DRESS | 133 |
| CUIRASSIER | 137 |
| A HEAVY SWELL—GUARD HUSSAR | 141 |
| A STUDY IN SOCIOLOGY IN BERLIN | 145 |
| THE OLD GENERAL | 149 |
| THE "SUB" | 153 |
| UHLAN OFFICER IN FIELD TRIM | 157 |
| THE OFFICERS' MESS | 161 |
| FIELD DRILL OF PRUSSIAN INFANTRY | 165 |
| AN OFFICER OF ARTILLERY | 169 |
| HUSSARS SCOUTING | 173 |
| AN OFFICER OF DRAGOONS IN THE FIELD | 176 |
| CAVALRYMAN WATERING HIS HORSE | 177 |
| A JOLLY PARTY BY THE WAYSIDE | 181 |
| A DRAGOON TRUMPETER | 185 |
| CUIRASSIER ON STAFF DUTY | 187 |
| TYPES OF PRUSSIAN OFFICERS | 190–191 |
| MOUNTED HUSSAR | 193 |
| ON THE ROAD TO TRAKEHNEN | 195 |
| COLTS PLAYING NEAR A HERD | 197 |
| MASSAGE OF A COLT'S KNEES | 201 |
| A "TRAKEHNER" HORSE-WRANGLER | 203 |
| BRINGING OUT A STALLION | 207 |
| THE RIDE THROUGH THE WOOD WITH THE OLD FORESTER | 211 |
| ARREST OF A POACHER IN THE FOREST | 215 |
| PEASANTS NEAR ROMINTEN | 219 |
| GERMAN PEASANT, EAST PRUSSIA | 222 |
| DEER AT ROMINTEN | 224 |
| THE EMPEROR'S HUNTING-LODGE | 227 |
| A FORESTER | 231 |
| A STALLION | 235 |

# THE BORDERLAND
## OF
# CZAR AND KAISER

### IN THE CZAR'S BARRACKS

MY friend Chumski, in the fatigue uniform of the 170th Infantry Regiment, met me at the station somewhere between Kasan and Moscow. He threw both arms about me, kissed me affectionately, led me to a carriage drawn by a pair of lively Arabs, and whirled me off to his quarters. Chumski is of Polish extraction, and commands the best regiment in Russia. This needs explanation, for it is well known that no Pole can rise beyond the grade of a captain unless he becomes so Russified in name, language, and religion as to pass for a good orthodox Slav. But Colonel Chumski is a rare man. His nationality has kept him from being a general, or commanding a regiment of the guards, but, on the other hand, his achievements in war have been so uniformly brilliant, the troops under him have shown such perfection of training, that when a Russian officer wants to compliment his men he can only say, "You are good enough for Chumski's regiment." The men of the 170th all love Chumski—first and foremost, because he does not steal. It seems odd to lay stress on this point, but to the private it makes all the difference in the world whether the regimental fund is spent on good food, or whether the colonel takes it with him to the card-table. Then, too, Chumski has spent much of his life in real war. He fought the campaign against Turkistan in 1867; in 1870 he helped at Samarcand; he was at Khiva in the campaign of 1873; at Khokan in 1875 and 1876; then in the great war against Turkey of 1877 and 1878. From that time down to the expedition to Penjdeh, in 1885, he was always in harness, fighting British interests in the far East, and learning the art of war in the best of all schools.

Said he to me once: "Do you know why Russia is so successful in her far Eastern warfare? It is because she sends out there, not her stupid Russians, but the quick-witted Poles, and others like them, whom she suspects of having 'ideas.' The Russian officers serve in Poland, the Polish officers on the Caspian and other remote posts, from which they could not return in time to help their country people in case of a revolution. That is true also of the privates, but not to so great an extent."

Speaking of *ideas*, reminds me that recently in Moscow a school-teacher asked a little girl to define the word *idea*. The child answered, naïvely, "An idea is what is opposed to the government!"

Chumski did not tell me, for he is a modest man, that the reason he was ordered to duty near the capital was that the government needed sadly men of his capacity to help get the army in fighting condition. (It may be as well to add here, in parenthesis, that I am concealing every detail that can identify my friend.)

I was pining for sleep when I arrived, and therefore, after a cup of coffee and a roll, lay down on a couch and was soon sound asleep. When I awoke, after a couple of hours, three soldiers stood at the foot of my bed, motionless and silent. At first, with the sleep fog veiling my faculties, they appeared agents of the Third Section demanding my passports, and I have a confused idea of shuddering with the suspicion, "What if Chumski has been ordered to arrest me!" But after rubbing my eyes the situation clears up cheerfully. A Cossack is there with my mount; he is to escort me to the drill-ground. The two orderlies are to help me dress. One holds a basin, the other pours out water upon my hands in a manner that reminded me of China. After a scanty wash, they help me into my riding breeches and boots with a dexterity suggesting that the colonel himself looked upon dressing and undressing as eminently work for servants. At the door stood a four-year-old Cossack horse with training-lines as well as a curb rein; he was a beautiful animal, full of fire, a trifle larger than usual, and vastly better bred than those one sees in the troop. Chumski did me great honor in allowing me to ride this precious beast that was destined to serve as his best charger, and I was highly flattered, for it presupposed that he had formed a fair opinion of my horsemanship when we last rode together in the Peloponnesus. We mounted without loss of time, I signalled my Cossack to act as guide, and away we dashed at a gallop over the market-place, amid peasants, pottery, and cabbages, clattering across the long bridge over the Volga, and out into the open country. The Cossack and his horse were as one, but something like a clever nurse and a spoiled child. Each understands and loves the other, but neither completely under control. My orderly did not want

ADVANCE OF RUSSIAN INFANTRY

his horse to be a slave, and recognized perfectly that horses, like children, have their whims and humors, and must be coaxed and reasoned with, but rarely punished. The morning was fresh, our mounts also. They capered and danced and bounded from side to side, and acted as only horses can act whose masters have an excellent seat, light hands, and an indulgent disposition. The German troop horse is more perfectly trained, more steady; one may say that he resembles the German scholar in being thoroughly reliable, but rarely brilliant. No cavalry horse approaches the German in the qualities demanded for that branch of the service, as no students, the world over, equal those of Germany in power and perseverance. I was speaking of our mounts only as pleasant saddle-horses for an individual. My saddle, too, the regular troop saddle, was comfortable—more so than that of the German cavalry, but by no means so light or useful as the McClellan saddle of our service.

After half an hour's ride we reached a level space, three sides of which were flanked by two-story buildings — the barracks of the regiment. Colonel Chumski asked if I would like to inspect his regiment, which, of course, I was very glad to do. We rode together between their lines, and I had abundant proof that the men were sound and well cared for. They were then put through a series of tactical evolutions, which they performed as well as any guard regiment I have ever seen, after which the band broke into a march, and we had a little review, first by company and then by battalion front. The men were in campaign outfit, and made a most excellent impression on me. When a company preserved a particularly correct line, the colonel called to them an acknowledgment in Russian, upon which the whole company burst into a roar, which was to me unintelligible, but which Chumski said was a vote of thanks from the men. When a line displeased him he did not conceal his opinion of their performance, and the slovenly men were promptly berated by their officers; in one instance it seemed to me that a man received a blow on his cheek from the officer's sword guard. In any other regiment I should have noted a dozen blows. When the review was over, the colonel gave the signal, and the whole regiment started at the height of its speed, each man for himself, all rushing to quarters, not in a perfunctory quickstep, but so violently as to suggest that some great reward was awaiting each man at the end of his journey. As they rushed, they burst into a hurrah that sounded like the roar of the ocean on a coral reef.

When the rush had passed away, and we stood alone, I told him that I was amazed at the excellence of his regiment, and wished to see what the men could do individually. Accordingly an

A BOLD DRAGOON

order was given, and in a few minutes out marched a company in full campaign kit, carrying, however, not the real rifle, but one entirely of wood. I was now treated to an obstacle race, in which the field consisted of one company of the 170th. The course was about half a mile long, and in covering that distance the men had to jump into ditches six feet deep, climb up steep banks twelve feet high, crawl under beams, vault bars, pass a stream by walking along a narrow plank, leap hurdles, and finally scale a smooth plank wall about eight feet high by vaulting over its top. To follow the rapidly shifting movements of these one hundred men was as difficult as watching a circus with three rings going at once, and when the last man had finished the course, and the company formed in line before us, my eyes still danced with a panorama of legs and arms gyrating over parapets and lofty beams. Chumski said something to the men, and was immediately answered by a unanimous roar. I asked him what it all meant.

"Nothing," he said. ".I only told them they had done well, and they answered that they were glad to earn the colonel's approbation.

"You see," said he, "I have lived a great deal with soldiers when real war was going on, and I know that the soldier is a child. You know that children like a kind word now and then; they like to be patted on the head; they like to be admired; that encourages them. Very well; so it is with my men. They like me to admire and praise them; and they work very much better when I treat them as a father does a child. Of course I punish them too, for I must have discipline."

What struck me particularly about Chumski's troops was the enthusiasm with which they did their work. They took their obstacles as though participants in an athletic contest.

The men of this regiment wore boots that reached almost to the knees, green trousers tucked in loosely, and a round green forage-cap similar to that in the German army. Their tunic was not of green cloth, such as they wear in cold weather, but simply of coarse unbleached linen, sitting snug around the throat and falling to the cuff when the hand is at the man's side. It is a loose and comfortable garment for gymnastic exercise. I admired it later, when some of the regiment gave us an exhibition of military rowing. Their knapsacks were fastened on by two straps coming over the shoulders and fastening at the belt, thus not only relieving the weight behind, but relieving also that of the two cartridge-belts which hang at the belt in front. In general, all their equipment is copied from German models, and in war-time I can imagine many a blunder caused by mistaking German for Russian troops, particularly when the mist hangs over the

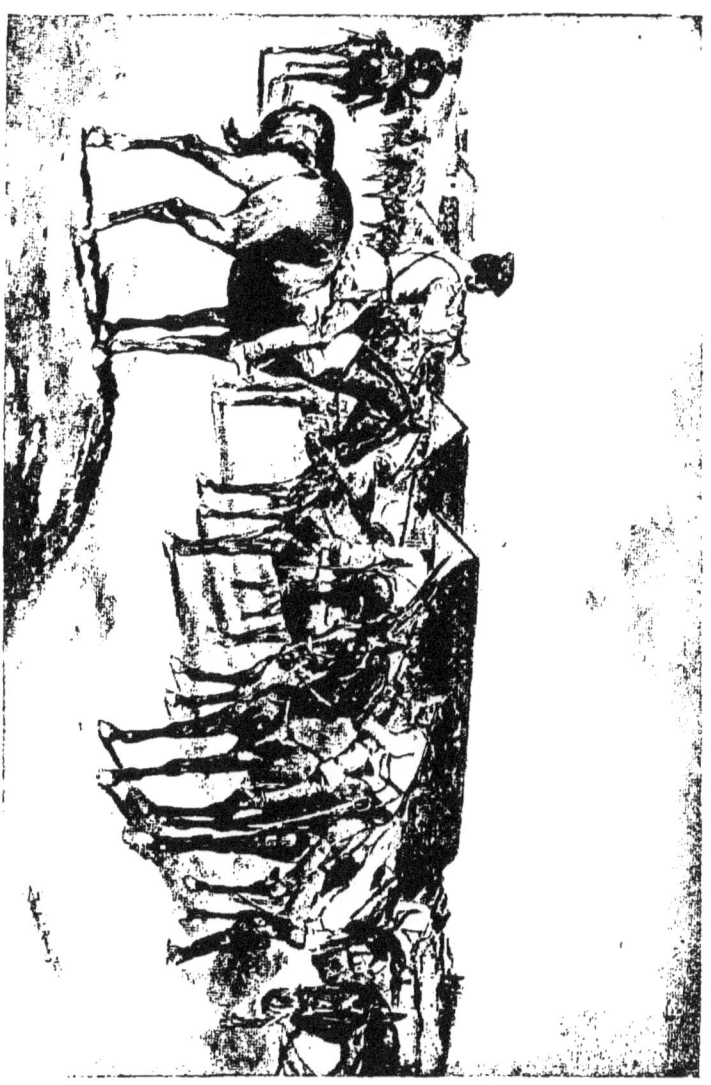

"DRAGOONS, MOUNT!"

meadows in the early morning. This applies only when the undress cap is worn. The Russian infantry head-piece is a round woolly hat, only high enough to clear the crown of the man's head, flat on top, with no rim or peak, and adorned in front with a brass double-headed eagle. The German's helmet seems to me better, in that it affords ventilation in hot weather, and sheds the rain from a man's neck. It also shields the eyes from the sun, if that be an advantage. The difference between the helmet and the woolly hat is practically the only one that separates the great body of Russian infantry from that of Germany.

"Shall we take a look at the barracks?" suggested the colonel. "Nothing would suit me better," I answered; so leaving our horses in charge of the Cossack, Chumski led the way through a series of vast spaces occupied mainly by little wooden beds. Each little bed had on it a hard mattress, a pillow, and a coarse woollen blanket. Beneath each bed was a box, in which the soldier's kit was kept, and at short intervals throughout the buildings were chromo portraits of the czar, and very gaudy pictures of Russian saints. The barracks were entirely of wood, the ceilings low, and the windows infrequent, yet so clean was everything kept that I detected no disagreeable odor. In the kitchen I helped myself to a taste of the soup that was simmering in vast caldrons over the brick oven, and made up my mind that I could stand a pretty long canoe cruise if my food were no worse than this. There are two fast-days in the week—Wednesday and Friday—and this was one of them, so that all they had was lentil soup. Black bread went with the soup—not such very bad bread either. They had a drink that suggested the mead we use at harvest-time, consisting of water in which rye bread has been absorbed. Of this I drank a whole glass with relish. So far, then, I had stumbled on nothing about the Russian soldier's life that would have discouraged me from enlisting had I been brought up to accept the czar's word as law.

"Do you have much desertion?" I asked.

"Not many in my regiment," answered the colonel, with complacency; "my men are pretty well cared for.

"But," said he, "the Jews have rather a rough time of it. I have about a hundred of them in this regiment, and they do their work as well as any of them. In most cases, however, they are exposed to much insult and brutality. Sometimes the soldiers beat them unmercifully, and it is no wonder that they try to desert. The rough peasant has a traditional hatred of the Jew, and if the officers of the regiment are not energetic in setting their faces against it, there is pretty sure to be some deviltry against them. The Russian

ONE OF THE CZAR'S BODY-GUARD

peasant finds it delightful to get even with the man whom he looks upon as the author of all his ills."

In the twenty-seven "governments" making up the western frontier of Russia, ten of which constitute Poland, the Jews are very much crowded together. In 1874 Russia followed Germany in adopting the principle of universal military service, and consequently forcing Jews into the army. The government has only published the statistics of desertion between 1876 and 1883, and for these years the number of Jew deserters in those districts amounted to a round 90,000 men. The government ceased then to publish such figures, but it is estimated that the number of Jews to-day who have run away from their regiments, or at least have failed to appear after passing the necessary physical tests, and after being ordered out—that this number is at least 150,000.

As we galloped home to the noon-day dinner, I noticed that my colonel greeted the men of other regiments than his own by merely conforming to the usual military requirements; but when he met any of his 170th, he shouted out a hearty good-day to them, which they answered with a burst of strange sound intended to convey the notion, "we are glad to have our colonel's greeting." This struck me as a very pleasant interchange of civility—much better than the silent and perfunctory ordeal in vogue among Western armies. In the German army the Emperor still greets his Grenadier Guards by a hearty "Good-morning," and is answered as heartily as in Russia; but this is in Germany as historically unique as the "beef-eaters" at the Tower of London. In Russia the life of the people is what it was in England when Queen Bess boxed the ears of her favorites—an odd medley of barbarism and parental gentleness.

Colonel Chumski made a splendid dinner in my honor. When he embraced me at our farewell meeting in the shadow of Mars Hill, he promised me all sorts of good things in case I came to Russia, and he more than kept his word. Half a dozen of his officers were present, most of them with either German or Polish names, and half of them speaking either French or German. Three orderlies in top-boots and linen tunics served us with a series of luxuries, commencing with a variety of cold relishes, such as caviare, pickled salmon, anchovy, cucumber, chopped egg, and several kinds of native whiskey. The courses succeeded each other as with us, but as regards wine, pretty much the whole table was covered with bottles of choice brands from Madeira, the Crimea, Tokay, Bordeaux—everywhere but the Rhine. The host was a generous toast-master, and acted on the principle that the guest who left his table sober went away unsatis-

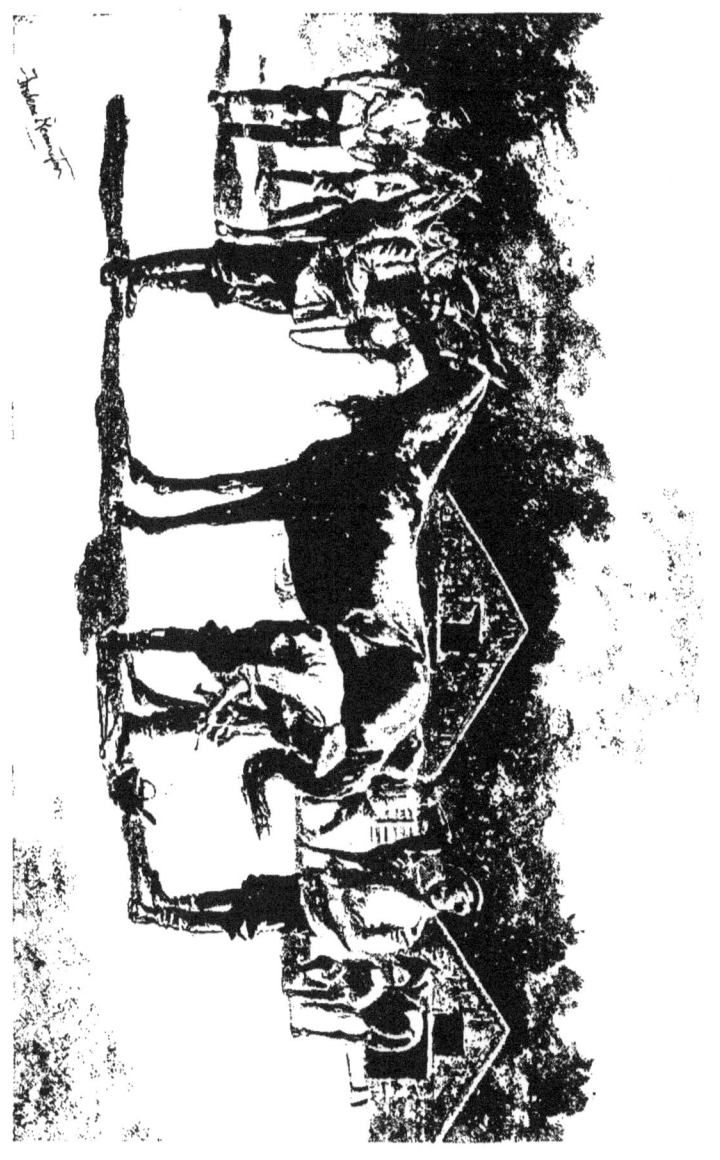

SHOEING COSSACK HORSES

fied. Personally, I am almost a total abstainer, and had some difficulty in finishing the meal without hurting the susceptibilities of my kind friends. There were a great many toasts offered, and much good feeling displayed, all of which is now merged in the memory of a pleasant meeting. After dinner we adjourned into the colonel's reception-room, in which were two great divans, on which we sat cross-legged, after the manner of Turks, smoked, chatted, and sipped coffee, prepared after the manner of the lower Danube and the East generally.

The colonel was very communicative now, though he was not reticent before. I attached some importance to his opinion, because he had not only seen his own troops in different campaigns, but knew European troops as well.

"That's a fine fellow, that Cossack," said I.

"Yes," answered Chumski; "the best stuff we have. Pity we have not more." After his other guests had retired, he took up the subject once more, and said: "The Russian is a poor horseman, and drill cannot make a cavalryman. Horses are cheap and abundant, yet we never ride unless we are forced to. The Cossack is otherwise; he loves his horse, he is full of resources, and is worth all the rest of the cavalry put together. Our cavalry of the guard is very showy and well trained, but I prefer the Cossack for my purposes."

Of the guard cavalry there is very little that corresponds to Chumski's description, however. The so-called Chevalier Garde corresponds to the famous Lifeguards of London, who attract all the nursery-maids of St. James and Whitehall when they solemnly move in and out of their strange sentry-boxes. They wear a double-headed silver eagle perched with outspread wings over a gilded helmet; have gilded breastplate, blue-gray trousers, and enormous boots. On festive occasions their tunic is white, but ordinarily dark green. In the whole Russian army there are, however, only four cuirassier regiments, and these are all stationed, for parade purposes, in or near the capital. Then there are two regiments of hussars, similar to the German, one red and the other green, and two regiments of uhlans, also easily mistaken for German. These are the only cavalry regiments that are showy and at the same time strikingly like those of Germany. The bulk of the Russian, as of the American cavalry, is composed of dragoons, who wear a peculiar head-piece, part fur, part cloth, with the metal double eagle at the front, readily distinguishable from the fur hat of the Cossack, which does not show so much fur in front. The fifty odd dragoon regiments of the Russian army, like ours, expect to fight afoot as well as in the saddle; are drilled to attack in masses, but at the same time do their best to emulate the peculiar virtues of the

COSSACKS SCOUTING

Cossack. Remington and I passed two squadrons of these dragoons quartered in a string of dirty peasant huts, about five miles from the Prussian frontier. Their horses were excellent in build and condition, and the men looked like good rough-and-ready skirmishers, but there was no ground near the place where any other tactics could have been practised save dismounting and attacking from behind trees. This explains, perhaps, why to-day so much of the cavalry in Poland is composed of material which, in Germany, would be considered fit only for scouting.

"You Americans like rough-and-ready fighting," said the colonel, "and I will show you some this afternoon, if you like a hard ride." This was delightful. The wine had evidently made him confiding as well as communicative. He clapped his hands, ordered horses, took a last glass of vodka, and in a few moments we were clattering out into the lonesome country, with the Cossack orderly behind.

There is nothing much sadder than Russia, and Remington's reference to it once as "the sad gray land" seemed more and more apt the more I saw of this mournful empire. I have seen it in the merry harvest-time and again in early June, the seasons when the rest of the world does most of its smiling and singing. The Russian peasants that have crossed my path, whether on the Black Sea or the Baltic, in St. Petersburg or the great Minsk Swamp, have struck me as being peculiarly like neglected cattle, having "neither pride of ancestry nor hope of posterity;" they look like people who have no change of clothing, and care for none; who are so attached to the soil that they like it even next to the skin; their dress takes the color of the land they till, and when Russian peasants stop in the fields to rest, the color blends with the surrounding features as does that of a partridge in a field of stubble.

My meditations were disturbed by the sound of rifle-firing. "What is that?" I asked. "Our scouts," answered the colonel. "Follow me," and he led the way as rapidly as practicable off the main road in the direction of the sound we had heard. At first it was difficult moving, owing to the branches and underbrush, but soon we struck a forest trail, and went ahead at a good trot. A cheer greeted our ears, and we soon afterwards came upon twenty soldiers, in command of Lieutenant Schützenberg, busily occupied in taking the insides out of a brown bear, preparatory to carrying him off with them. A sapling was cut down and trimmed of its branches, and on this Bruin was swung. The green-coated scouts then tramped off into the woods in the opposite direction from that in which we had come. Soon I noticed, here and there between the trees, single figures of soldiers who surround-

THE SOLDIERS' SONG

ed the little column at a distance, in order to give warning in case of danger.

Lieutenant Schützenberg saluted the colonel, we dismounted and walked with him behind the bear-carriers, while I learned from their commander something of this operation.

In the German army every soldier is taught to act intelligently on outpost service and in scouting operations, and this is not too much to require in a country where every soldier reads and writes, and can readily understand a map and compass. In Russia, however, where nine-tenths of the people cannot read or write, and have lost the faculty of thinking consecutively, the army cannot teach the soldier much more than to move as with a machine. In order to have a force of good men for picket-work and advance-skirmishing, they have adopted this plan:

Each company sends four of its most intelligent men to a select body called the scouting-corps, and as the Russian regiment has four battalions, with four companies each, that gives a regimental scout force of sixty-four. This service is very popular, for it is full of variety, and though the hardship is great, the food is good, for hunting and fishing are in the programme. The men are practised in every kind of wood-craft, and are expected to develop as much ingenuity and self-reliance as an Indian scout in our service. They must sail, row, swim, climb, find their way by map and compass, slip through the enemy's lines, procure every variety of information, and escape capture at all hazards.

"They are splendid fellows," said Schützenberg, in answer to a question of mine. "Here is what they did last winter when snow was on the ground and floating ice in the streams:

"You must know that we attach very great importance to creeping up close to the enemy and watching his movements. Well, for a little practice in this respect I called my sixty-four men together one morning in the barrack-yard, and divided them into two sides, each commanded by non-commissioned officers. I pointed out on the map a position which one side was to watch, and indicated the direction from which an attack was to be anticipated. Another position I selected for the other side. Neither side knew what the other side was to attempt, but each had orders to slip behind the lines of the other, and steal three flags that had been posted about a mile and a half in the rear of the line that was to be protected. The difficult part of the problem was that neither side knew anything of the positions beyond what was shown them on the map in the barrack-yard, and the non-commissioned officers had to transmit this knowledge to their men.

"Each party found the right position, and after posting sentry, detached a party to steal the flags

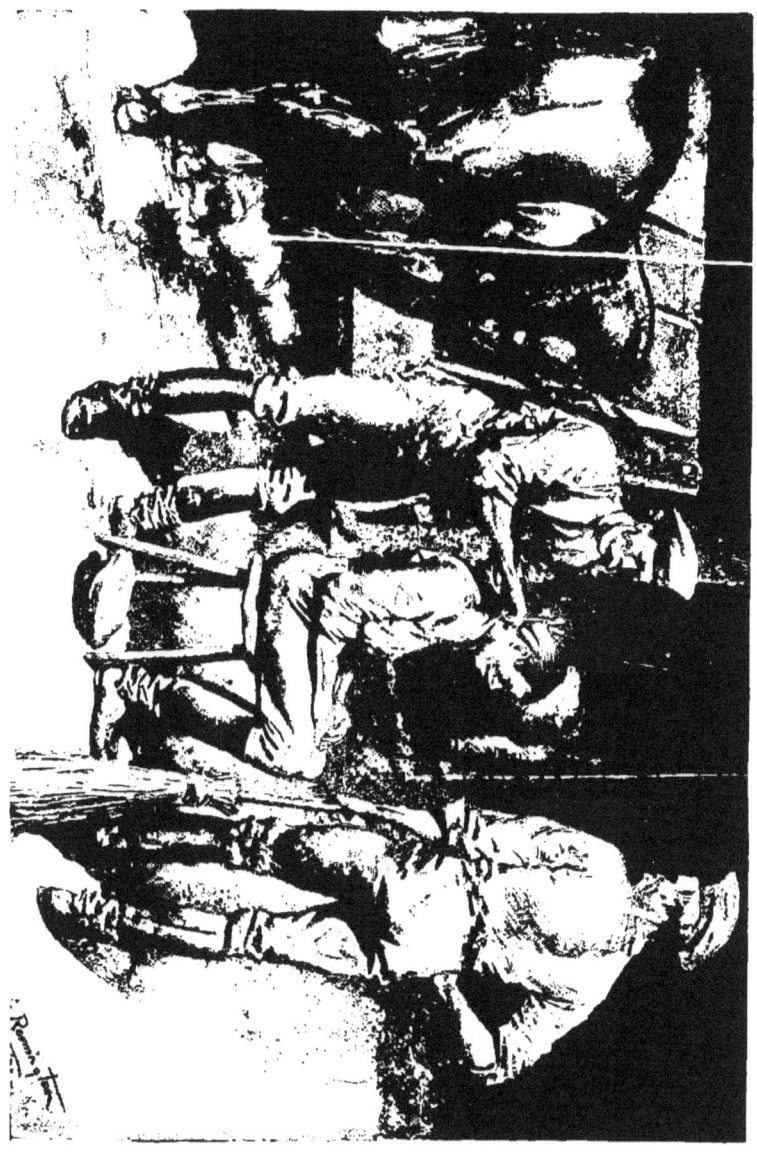

A HAIR-CUT IN A CAVALRY STABLE

of the enemy. Six men of the one party went off, each on his own account. Two of them were captured, one of them failed to find the flags because he could not remember the topography of the map, and one succeeded in finding the flags and bringing them back to the noncommissioned officer. The remaining two found the spot after the flags were gone, and described it, so that there was no doubt that they had been there. The six men detailed on the other side for the work remained together, and were discovered when close to the picket line. They were fired upon; two were captured, and the remaining four pursued to a stream forty feet wide near here. In spite of the floating ice, they sprang in and struggled to the other side. The pursuers hesitated a moment at the sight of the ice-blocks, then they followed. One was captured in the water because he was hampered by the ice. The rest escaped; but one of the followers managed, in spite of his ice bath, to sneak away with the flags of the enemy.

"They are invaluable to us," said Schützenberg, enthusiastically; "and for our country as good as cavalry when it comes to reconnoissance. For what can cavalry do in forest and swamp and on boggy roads?

"Last summer a scout corps of the 6th Orenburg Cossacks covered in two months 1800 versts (a verst is about five-sixths of a mile), most of the distance being rough country, without roads of any kind, over glaciers and across rapid streams. This was the famous Pamir expedition, from which the scout corps returned in excellent health.

"Pamir is close to the British India line," added Schützenberg, with a sly wink, "and we are constantly sending out 'scientific' expeditions to explore the borders of our uncertain neighbors."

The so-called scientific expeditions of Russia are, as is well known, only so in name. They are merely military reconnoissances, with just enough science about them to bring back to the war department a rough idea of what the territory would be worth if annexed to the empire.

Pretty soon our conversation was interrupted by shouts behind us, and a dozen of the scout corps came crashing through the thicket in hot pursuit of those who had shot the bear. Their top-boots were coated with mud, and for that matter they nearly all showed that they had done some heavy floundering in the swamp. They carried their rifles like practised hunters, and followed the enemy with energy, hoping to capture some of them before they reached the Volga. We let them pass, then followed in their wake. I was thoroughly roused. It seemed as though I was taking part in a most exciting game; and

KUBAN COSSACK, IMPERIAL GUARD CORPS.

for that matter there was a huge stake in this race—namely, the big brown bear; for the winners would most certainly bag the bear. On we went, crashing through the underbrush, floundering in swamp, now and then getting a trot on hard bottom. The pursuers showed excellent grit, and that rare quality designated by Remington as "sporting blood." But they lost the stake, for when we emerged on the river-bank we saw the other party sailing away home in a big boat—in fact, they were already skinning their booty. When they saw their discomfited pursuers they set up a roar of triumphant cheering, which fell on our ears as the news of a great calamity. There was a great feast in the regiment that night, and the big brown bear disappeared under many savory disguises and amid many bottles of excellent wine. The skin was presented to me by the colonel of the regiment amid most friendly expressions, and will always remind me of several sturdy Russian soldiers, who made me for a time forget that I was under police supervision.

As we rode home towards evening I asked the colonel a little in detail about the Russian scout corps.

"Here is an outfit," said he: "A sail-boat with 2 masts, holding 18 people; 2 row-boats, each holding a dozen; 5 bicycles, 10 heavy sporting-rifles, 10 compasses, 20 pairs of snow-shoes, 30 pairs of skates, a large fishing-net, and good winter outfit for 64 men."

"Do you call that your museum?" I asked, "or am I to understand that you give your scout company a thorough all-round athletic training?"

"This regiment does not run a museum," answered the colonel. "Far from it. Every article I have enumerated represents a means of special training. To-day the sporting-rifles, compasses, maps, and boats were practised. We do a great deal of sailing and rowing, for a good sailor makes a good rough-and-ready man at anything. When the roads are good, we practise despatch-carrying on bicycles.

"Then we have splendid fishing all about here, and in a campaign men should know how to provide for their mess. In winter we track on snow-shoes, and skate wherever possible. But bear-hunting is, after all, the main sport. My men learn more at bear-hunting than in the barrack-yard, and when I command troops I always look to my bear-hunters."

Of course the training which the scout corps gets varies with the climate and the physical nature of the country. Every regiment has not the water needful for its navy, and skating cannot be indulged in towards the South. But the principle of instruction is the same, whether in Finland or Turkistan, Poland or Siberia. The scout

THE RUSSIAN MILITARY GENDARME

corps devotes itself to every form of athletic exercise that can make its men valuable in a scouting campaign, and that can give it the special education that will enable it to support itself when separate from its base.

"European people are so conceited," said Chumski, "that they do not know what we are doing in the midst of this stagnant population of peasants. The scout company of sixty-four men that I have here is just the sort of stuff that General Sherman could have appreciated in his famous march to the sea; it is just the stuff that made the famous march from Boston to Quebec in the winter of 1775 and '76; it is just the stuff that Napoleon should have had in 1812, when he tried to march half a million men from Paris to Moscow."

As we walked our horses slowly homeward in the twilight after our pretty stiff day's work, we caught now and then on the still air the sound of men chanting in unison, then the tramp, tramp of soldiers, and finally the gray outline of a company of the 170th, who were taking their regular evening outing before retiring to bed. The colonel gave them a hearty good-evening; the singing stopped, and instead came a series of shouts that burst in unison with the marching time, and meant that the men returned the compliment. Then the melancholy song once more commenced, and the gray column disappeared in the dusty dimness of the setting sun.

Chumski roused me from my brooding by saying: "I think that Russia has the simplest and most useful field uniform in Europe; much more so than Germany. The emperor Alexander III. introduced a complete change in the uniforming of our men—first, out of economy; secondly, in order to make the national costume more popular. Green is our national color, as blue is that of Germany, and red that of England. Our national green is seen not only on the backs and heads of all our infantry, but on the trousers as well, the only other color being the distinguishing bits at the shoulder and collar and cap band to mark regiments or ranks."

One exception I had noted at the Roumanian border, and again on that of Lithuania, the ever-watchful frontier patrol, which is distinguished from the rest of the army by having gray-blue trousers, a double row of brass buttons down the front, and only one cartridge-box at the belt instead of two. I took a good look at those fellows when I first met them, and shall not soon forget them.

"Buttons are a nuisance," said the colonel. "They have to be cleaned, they wear away the cloth, they are heavy, they attract the attention of the enemy. Our infantry has abolished them everywhere but on the frontier patrol, and there

ONE OF THE CZAR'S PIRATES
From a sketch made in St. Petersburg

they still remain, I suppose because those fellows do police duty, and must look impressive. Our tunic folds over the breast, and is fastened by five hooks and eyes that are not seen and do not catch in everything. The Germans are too fond of show. They should have discarded buttons long ago.

"Our cavalry has more latitude in matter of uniform, yet the great bulk of it are dragoons who wear green coats, green caps, and gray-blue trousers something like those of the United States army. The Astrakhan Cossack, the Don Cossack, the Ural Cossack — these are all blue, and there are a few more varying uniforms, but taking the whole army there is very little difference between the men of one corps and those of another. The artillery, engineers, scouts, all wear the complete green dress, and their overcoat is the historic gray, very loose, very long, very warm. People outside have an idea that we have a horde of gorgeous, barbarous cavalry in theatrical dress. This is a mistake. They are barbarous enough, I admit, but their uniform is now pretty tame everywhere. The emperor still keeps his so-called body-guard or imperial escort in a native savage dress, with high fur hat, red or brown coat, with cartridge-cases across the chest.

"The Kuban Cossacks are like them, with horrible knives in their belt, a rifle in a shaggy fur case strung over their shoulder, and a general appearance of having just come from some butchering expedition in central Asia."

Remington and I noted a number of those fellows about St. Petersburg, and made up our minds that between nihilists and Amoor Cossacks we preferred the nihilists. If the President of the United States should invite a band of Apaches to constitute his body-guard, we might get some notion of the incongruity as it struck us in St. Petersburg.

# WHY WE LEFT RUSSIA

## I

IT was on the railway between Alexandrowo and Warsaw. Remington and I had secured a compartment to ourselves, and were looking forward to a comfortable rest, stretched each upon a soft seat. We were on the "express," which in Russia means a train that does not carry cattle, and occasionally attains a speed of twenty-five miles an hour. Shortly after leaving the German frontier a tall bearded official, wearing an Astrakhan hat, loose trousers tucked into long boots, and a tunic belted at the waist, threw open our door with startling swiftness. He stood still for a moment, observing us intently; then consulted a piece of paper he held in his hand, looked once more keenly at me, then turned and said a few words to a similarly dressed man behind him, who had been hidden from us by the door of the compartment, but who now came forward and assisted in the scrutiny.

Under the circumstances we could not but regard their behavior as an act of impertinence, for each of us bore a document technically known as "special passport," issued by our government only to accredited agents and such as are particularly vouched for. This document was signed by the ex-Secretary of State James G. Blaine on March 4, 1892, and was a request "to permit [the bearer] to pass freely without let or molestation, and to extend to him all such friendly aid and protection as would be extended to like citizens of foreign governments resorting to the United States."

I had also a second passport with me, which included my wife. That was, however, only the ordinary passport, which invoked not *friendly aid and protection*, but simply "lawful aid and protection."

As the bearded official continued his scrutiny, we sought to pretend indifference, and handed our tickets, which were accepted in a mechanical manner. The door was slammed, and we were once more alone.

Neither of us relished the episode, for we were travelling on a legitimate errand, and had taken special pains to establish our identity in the proper quarters. The United States government had commissioned me to make a report upon the best means of protecting our sea-coast against the ravages of wind and waves, and my orders were to note particularly what had been done along the sandy shores of the Baltic, where the conditions suggest very strongly our shores of Long Island and New Jersey.

THE THIRD SECTION AT WORK

"What do you suppose that fellow wanted of us?" queried Remington.

"A ruble," said I; "and we've got the best of him;" with which comprehensive answer I began to roll my jacket up for a pillow.

"That won't do," said Remington, after a pause. "That fellow with the beard had more than a ruble's worth of scowl on him. He was comparing you with his paper. You've grown a beard since your last passport."

"That's none of his business," I answered.

To be sure, I had grown a beard during the winter, because I had torn a finger to pieces while experimenting with a cog-wheel. But I could not see why the police should care about that.

"At any rate," continued Remington, with emphasis, "that fellow with the beard is going to make us trouble. I feel it down in my bones. I don't mind being shot, but I do hate sitting still in prison. Good-night."

II

The train rumbled into Warsaw. Remington and I handed our valises to the porter of the hotel, but, instead of taking the omnibus or cab, slipped out through the crowd, and, with the aid of a map, strolled about the streets to take a look at the town before reporting at the hotel.

In Paris I had made the acquaintance of a very intelligent Polish landed proprietor, and had promised to look him up. The address he had given me in Warsaw was that of a German chemist in a large drug-shop. I was to ask for Mr. X., and introduce myself—the rest I was to leave to him.

This seemed an odd way of accomplishing a simple and innocent visit, but there was no other. We entered the drug-store; pretended to need a tooth-brush; asked casually for Mr. X.; he appeared from a back room; I pretended to want something chemical, and when out of ear-shot, asked after my friend. The manner of Mr. X. immediately changed; he took me into his back room, leaving Remington to inspect tooth-brushes, and after satisfying himself that I was the party I pretended to be, said, anxiously,

" Have you been to your hotel yet?"

I said no.

"That is right," said he, somewhat relieved. " Are you sure that no one has tracked you from the station to this door?"

I told him how we had disposed of our luggage, how we had slipped through the crowd, and expressed the opinion that if any one had kept an eye on us during the railway journey, he certainly could not have followed us to his door without our knowledge.

" You did well," he said, " but still you had

better not call on Mr. Zerowski," for that was my friend's name. "You had better go to your hotel now, for if you stay longer away, it will excite suspicion. Say nothing while a servant is in the room. If you have any papers you don't wish read, carry them on your person. A police spy will come to your room five minutes after you have surrendered your passport. He will pretend to be an American, or at least to have lived in America and to love Americans. He will want to find out what you have done and what you propose doing, and will see that you are watched. While you are out he will see that your luggage is searched; you had better lock nothing up. Tell him you leave early to-morrow morning for St. Petersburg, and must have your passports back; promise him a ruble, to have no mistake. Then drop in at the Café Tomboff at exactly 3.50, but do not act as though you looked for any one there. Zerowski will join you five minutes later, quite by accident, you understand. Good-bye."

### III

Remington and I looked at each other dubiously as we left the chemist and sought our hotel. Neither of us relished the idea of attaining our object by indirect methods, although I was prepared to sacrifice something for the sake of exchanging news with my Polish friend Zerowski, who, by-the-way, makes it his business to know what is going on.

"I don't care for Russia, anyway," said Remington, finally, after we had spent some minutes debating the advisability of joining Zerowski at the Café Tomboff. "Let's go back to Germany, Hungary, Turkey, Africa—anywhere out of this—"

He did not finish his sentence, for at that point the door opened softly and swiftly to admit a sleek little bald-headed, black-coated, blinking man of about fifty years of age, who said, with a smirk, and in bad English, "I thought I heard you say 'Come in !'"

We had not said "Come in," but did not discuss that point.

"You have just arrived from Berlin?" he said.

"No, from America," said Remington.

"But where did you stop last before reaching Warsaw?"

"Wherever the train stopped," said Remington.

He then tried to know where our next objective was, whether we had friends in Warsaw, how long we should stop, and finally offered himself to us as guide, philosopher, and friend, on the strength of having lost his heart in America.

We parried his questions, gave him to under-

"I THOUGHT I HEARD YOU SAY 'COME IN!'"

stand that we did not need him, expelled him finally from the room, and then strolled off to the Café Tomboff.

The chemist was right; the spy was in our wake. We had scarcely seated ourselves at the Tomboff when the little blinking man entered the place, took his seat at a table in the corner, and engaged in earnest conversation with a guest who had been sipping a cup of coffee there. The subject of the conversation was obviously ourselves, to judge by the manner in which the second man's eyes worked in our direction. The blinking man soon disappeared, and the younger one was left to watch.

Zerowski entered the outer door of the Tomboff exactly five minutes after Remington and I had taken our seats. He stood a moment on the threshold, in the manner of a man undecided whether to loaf or go to work. His eyes rested on us, then on the spy, then wandered listlessly about the room. Finally, pretending to be very much bored, he sauntered down among the little tables, passed ours without a glance at me, went slowly to the farthest end of the establishment, appeared very much annoyed at not finding a table for himself alone, strolled back towards us, asked politely if he might sit at our table, took his seat as a stranger, offered Remington a cigarette, and said to me, in a whisper, as he bowed to Remington:

"Consider that I've never seen you before; there is an agent of the secret service three tables from you."

Zerowski is one of the many patriots in Poland who remain in their own country, bound by large estates which they cannot dispose of, and who pray morning and night for a cessation of the present barbarous government. Like most Poles with a liberal education, he has served a term in the Warsaw citadel, and is on the list of "suspects" who are to be arrested and deported at the first rumblings of revolution in Poland.

"What is the news?" I asked.

"Don't ask me," he said, "we are in Russia, in the Military Department of the Vistula." Then lowering his voice, he said, in French: "There will be soon another excursion to Siberia — a large one this time—students of the university here—you should stop to see it—in about seventy days, I think."

Remington, whose senses have been quickened by mixing paints among the huts of Cheyennes and Apaches, gave me at this point a kick beneath the table-cloth, and remarked, with emphasis, that he did not relish the company of the sneak-agent, who by this time had brought his chair one table nearer.

"I shall go from here to the theatre," said Zerowski; "shall get three seats together; shall send two by a safe messenger to your hotel; they

IN THE CAFÉ TOMBOFF

will be there in an hour; meanwhile stroll about town, and let the hotel porter know where you are going, so as to disarm suspicion."

The theatre was full; but as neither Remington nor I included Polish among our acquired accomplishments, we could not do justice to the performance.

Zerowski came in, but took a seat far away from us, in spite of the fact that the seat next to me remained vacant. After the first act we met in the adjoining garden, and his first words were:

"Thank God, the scoundrel has gone! He saw that I took a seat far from you. He concludes that he can make nothing of us to-night. He has gone to write his report, or do some other dirty work."

"But about the university?" I asked.

"Not a word has appeared or can appear in any Russian paper; not a word can pass the censor that touches this matter. I have a 'discreet' friend in the Warsaw faculty; he has told me something, but it would mean dismissal or worse to him if the police knew that he had said a word about it.

"You must know," said Zerowski, "that the czar's government has undertaken to tear up by the roots every manifestation of life that does not spring from soil prepared by Russian priest or police. The little veneer of civilization you find in Russia is due to Poland in the first place, and, in modern times, to Germany. I am a Pole. My family had enjoyed the fruits of European civilization hundreds of years before Russia emerged from a wilderness of prowling Cossacks. The Russian hates us because he is grossly inferior intellectually, and because we refuse to descend to his level. He has conquered us; he has flogged us; he has erased the name of Poland from his map. My children dare not speak their mother-tongue; my wife dares not employ a governess of her own nation; my very servants must be selected for me by the Russian police. The czar has cut Poland off from all intercourse with Europe, and forced her to starve or pick up the crumbs from his table. The Pole can no longer get a decent education in his own country; the Russian police control our schools as they do our newspapers, and their object is to have all the professions in Poland filled only by orthodox Russians.

"People in England and America cannot understand what this means, for superficially it seems a light burden. But look at it from the Polish side. You are a young man. You wish to become an engineer, a doctor, a lawyer, an architect — anything of that kind. You must pass a series of government examinations, or you cannot begin to earn a living. Your examiners are Russians, and they have orders to favor all the 'Orthodox,' and place obstacles in the way of Poles. Suppose, after passing all the preliminary obstacles, you get your government license, you find then that you can accomplish everything if you are of the Greek Church, and next to nothing if you are not. In Russia the government permeates every department of human activity — military, medical, legal, administrative, telegraph, railway, engineering. You cannot place your finger on anything that does not depend to a large extent upon government favor. As a result you find that at every step in your professional course you are heavily handicapped by the knowledge that you will never get employment except from the very few who are so bold as to employ you in spite of your national disability. Poles do still earn a living, but it is mainly by making themselves exceptionally useful to a Russian official who has more patronage than intelligence. A few days before you arrived the Polish students at the Warsaw University had been deeply outraged by the Russian head of the faculty — or rather, I should say that a series of outrages brought on an explosion. The Russians, one and all, stupid or not, received diplomas at Commencement; while the Poles, whose capacity was notoriously superior, were, almost to a man, rejected. The shameless political bias was so apparent that all Warsaw was ablaze, and one fine day the students lost control of themselves, and gave the three most obnoxious members of their faculty a sound pelting. Such a thing probably never could happen in America—"

To which I was compelled to answer that I had known, " 'neath the elms of dear old Yale," of students smashing the window of a *very* unpopular tutor.

" Bismarck used to pretend that the Poles were like the Irish — chronically rebellious. That is not true. There is no similarity between the two nations. England is giving Ireland the best government that unhappy country has ever had; Russia is giving Poland the worst government it is possible to conceive of—worse even than what she gives her own orthodox subjects. England is raising the Irish to a higher level; Russia is dragging us down into the mud."

" What will the police do with the disorderly Polish students?" I asked.

" Not so loud, if you please," said Zerowski, glancing about him. " There are spies at work now. They are being watched. The meshes are being drawn slowly and silently about them. Their letters are intercepted. They are being lulled into a false sense of security. By-and-by, in about three months, a raid will be made, and another transport to Siberia commence. . . ."

Between the acts we met by accident Professor X., the Polish member of the faculty, to whom Zerowski introduced us.

A GENDARME IN WARSAW

"Ask him about the university row," whispered my friend to me.

I did so, and Professor X. answered with ostentatious emphasis:

"University row! You surely must be thinking of some other university! The Warsaw University never has any row of any kind! Good-evening."

Zerowski smiled sadly as the form of the professor disappeared in the crowd.

"There goes," said he, "a product of Russian rule—the smooth liar. That is the man who told me the whole story. I introduced you only to give you a little object-lesson."

As we parted that night, Zerowski said: "You will understand why it is better that I do not come to the station to see you off. You are being watched here, and you will not move in Russia without a police agent behind you."

## IV

On the 6th of June Remington and I reached St. Petersburg, and after depositing our scant canoe kit at the hotel, hurried to the legation of the United States.

The St. Petersburg cabs have wheels a trifle larger than that of a wheelbarrow, and hold about as much. Remington and I hugged each other hard to keep from "dripping out" over the sides as we jumped and bumped over the rough pavement of the vast and lonesome squares that seem specially designed for military purposes. The horse of the droschka is small but spry, and drags the clumsy little cab with extraordinary facility. Every other cab we met contained a man in uniform. Germany seemed bad enough in this respect, but in St. Petersburg there seemed no choice between uniforms and rags. The driver, no doubt, likes the small droschka because it makes his horse look stronger, while the official, no doubt, loves it because it makes his proportions appear to advantage. The horse probably curses it as a clumsy weight, and sighs for a civilized carriage.

A most distinguished-looking footman opened the door for us, in answer to our ring, and ushered us into a room full of costly adornment. The legations of Berlin, Paris, London, and Vienna paled in comparison with this princely suite, for from our seats we gazed in wonder upon room after room of corresponding luxury.

Being but plain American travellers, and having been ushered into this apartment in answer to our desire to speak with our representative, we concluded that we were in the office of the United States, and that an extra appropriation had been made to defray the expense of this mission. But we were wrong.

There was no United States minister in St. Petersburg when we called, and the first secretary, who acted as chargé, informed us that we were in his private residence, one room of which appeared especially reserved for office purposes.

In other countries, particularly semi-civilized ones, the American seeking the protection or assistance of his minister is cheered by the sight of the American eagle over the legation door, possibly by a flag-staff from which the stars and stripes wave proudly on national holidays, proclaiming to all the world that wherever the American citizen travels he is sure of the support of his government so long as he obeys the laws of the place in which he is sojourning. But even if eagle and banner are absent, there is, in any event, a small brass plate affixed in some conspicuous place, with the information that there is such a thing as a legation of the United States in the place.

In St. Petersburg Remington and I looked in vain for some such cheering sign. There may have been one in Russian, but few American travellers speak that language. We stumbled about in a wretchedly homesick condition, ringing all the bells in the neighborhood, finding no one who could speak our language, and at length stumbling by accident upon the door of the magnificent gentleman who represents the government of Washington near the person of our friend the Czar of all the Russias. I had sent a letter on the first day of June, informing our chargé in St. Petersburg that I bore a commission from the United States government, that I bore also the "special passport" of the State Department, and in addition an official letter from the Secretary of State introducing me personally to our diplomatic agents abroad.

Remington also bore the "special passport," and I added in my letter that he and I were travelling together in order more completely to fulfil the wishes of our government.

Mindful of the rapidity with which the average American diplomatist loses sight of his native land in the midst of courtly pomp, I took the occasion to remark that my companion was, in his line, the first artist of America, and desired permission to make sketches.

My letter remarked also that we had, at considerable cost, brought with us from America each a cruising canoe, that we proposed sailing from St. Petersburg the whole length of the Baltic, making notes and sketches as we went along.

Finally, I begged that our representative in St. Petersburg procure for me the necessary permission to make this cruise, or else, at least, present me to the official of whom I might make the request in person, and explain the innocent nature of our proposed trip.

SCENE IN A POLISH VILLAGE

Knowing the delays of diplomacy in Eastern and semi-civilized countries, I suggested the 8th of June as the day of presentation, assuring the American chargé that we should certainly be on hand before then.

Remington and I had racked our brains to imagine what further we could do to divest our mission of suspicious circumstance. We at last concluded to add a protocol to our document—to wit, we offered to pay the expenses of any one the Russian government should kindly send along with us as interpreter, guide, pilot, protector, or spy.

We knew that last year the United States government had sent a special committee to Russia to report upon Jewish emigration, that this committee had been snubbed, and that it left St. Petersburg in disgust, without having been recognized by the proper department of state.

Against this contingency we fancied we had protected ourselves completely, for we had sent our request a week beforehand. Our mission was not in the remotest degree connected with any political question whatsoever; for what can be more innocent than the question of tree-planting along the sea-shores?

Besides, I had made a full statement of my purpose to the much-beloved ambassador of Russia in Berlin, Count Schuvaloff. He is a man full of amiability, particularly kind to Americans, and incapable of guile. He could not have shown more interest in my project had he been my own father; assured me that I would have a delightful trip, that I should be received with open arms, begged to know what he could do for me, even gave me a most cordial letter of introduction to one of the greatest names in St. Petersburg.

What more could an American citizen desire, travelling in a country bound to us by so many friendly ties as Russia? Surely we did not expect the American navy as escort! The fleet of grain-ships which we sent for the starving peasants should have been a good substitute.

The American chargé calmly informed us at our first interview that he had not made any request, written or oral, in our behalf.

This was rather staggering, after giving him a week's start for this very purpose! Remington looked ready for a fight.

The chargé explained that there was some difficulty in regard to diplomatic usage or precedent.

I protested that the Russian minister in Washington would find no difficulty in getting his request before the Secretary of State, and I ventured to think that the United States minister in St. Petersburg was of quite as much importance as the Russian minister in Washington, and that if that was not the case, it was time people in

America heard all about it. Our formal papers we had brought along, and asked him to read them. He did so, returned them, and remarked, in rather a tired manner, that they were lacking in diplomatic form.

To this I rejoined that it was not for me to criticise the diplomatic form of my State Department; that he might do that if he chose, but not through me. That our business in St. Petersburg was exclusively to obtain such permission as should protect us in our coasting cruise.

The chargé answered very vaguely, and reminded me that in the last year the Russian government had grown very jealous of foreigners who came to report upon things in Russia. To this I answered that China also disliked the foreigner, but that I had found no difficulty in travelling there—even into the interior.

We pressed upon him the fact that both of us were prepared to give the fullest guarantees regarding the purely innocent nature of our cruise. Again we offered to defray the cost of a government escort. The chargé smiled, and shook his head, and told us urbanely that we had come on a fool's errand.

Finally, in the presence of our military attaché and Remington, I said to him : " Here is a formal request. I ask you, on the strength of the government papers I carry, to take me before the proper official of the Russian government; I wish to be properly introduced to him; I wish to present the credentials of the United States government; I wish to explain the nature of our mission, and I wish to learn definitely from his lips whether there can possibly be any obstacle thrown in our path."

The chargé looked from one to the other of us with a quizzical smile. Had we asked for a loan of the Russian czar, I should have expected such a smile.

"It's quite impossible," was his terse answer. "It's contrary to all diplomatic precedent, don't you know!"

What was to be done? Remington and I concluded to wait at least three days. If by that time the government gave us no answer, we should take our canoes to the first German port, cruise the Kaiser's coast first, and then return to Russia, in case permission should have been finally accorded.

The chargé had at last condescended to promise that he would write formally for the needed authority, and would do everything in his power to further our mission, etc.

Russia is an expensive place to live in, particularly the capital. The stranger is fair game for extortion, and we found that at the rate of outlay current with us, we should soon be bankrupt. Socially our time passed agreeably enough, for we had letters to high and mighty functionaries, who treated us most cordially, invited us to their country-seats, offered to do everything under heaven to enhance our happiness, except the one thing we particularly wished done. Princes, counts, colonels, ambassadors, adjutants, and aides-de-camp—these could furnish caviar, champagne, and lordly hospitality, but not one of them dared move in a matter interesting to the Third Section—the secret police.

The letters we received were of course opened by the police, and clumsily closed again. Remington was one day driving in the suburbs, when he became aware that an official was following in a second droschka. The following droschka, however, passed his after a while, and Remington noticed that its occupant spoke to a gendarme on the road ahead. What he said, of course we do not know, but when Remington reached that point, the gendarme stopped his carriage, turned the horse's head back towards the city, and gave the driver some instructions in Russian that resulted in Remington finding himself an unwilling arrival back at the hotel, where I found him an hour later, pacing the floor like a caged lion, and venting his feelings in vigorous English.

We were used to being watched, but this was more than we had bargained for.

On the fourth day we called at the legation at half-past ten in the forenoon. The impressive man-servant told us that his excellency the chargé was in bed. We sent up word on a card that we called to know if he had any news for us. He sent down word by the splendid servant that he had no news; did not know when he should have any; that there was no use in our waiting for any.

We returned a farewell message of thanks and compliments, and left.

Two days before, we had interviewed the head of the customs, and had arranged to have our boats shipped by fast freight to Kovno, on the river Niemen, supposing that forty-eight hours' start was quite enough. We had also told the hotel porter that we were to start to-day, and ordered him to have our passports. He came to us with a drawn face, however; said he was very sorry; that he had been to the police station; that there was some difficulty; that he could not get them for us.

"Now we *are* in for it," thought we. For, of course, without a passport we ceased to be Americans, or even human beings; we became merely the number of a police cell.

Luckily for us, an official close to the person of the czar happened to call upon us at that moment, and to him we explained our predicament. He left us for a moment, then returned, and assured us that there must be some mistake, that our passports would surely arrive. We chatted

GENDARME, ST. PETERSBURG

for a while, and, sure enough, as though by magic, the precious documents once more made their appearance, duly stamped and sealed. What potent spell our great friend had exercised we shall never know, but to us he was a friend in need, and we feel very grateful for his intercession.

V

Between St. Petersburg and Kovno I stopped for a chat with a friend who knows the devious methods of Russian government pretty well. I told him my tale, and asked him what he made of it.

"Nothing is simpler," said he. "You are politely requested to disappear from Russia at the shortest possible notice. You have been watched from beginning to end, and you may be watched at this moment. You might have waited a month in St. Petersburg, but you would never have got an answer to your request."

"But," said I, "what if I had gone on without permission?"

"You would never know what had interfered with you. You would have been arrested at the first convenient place, and kept a week or so pending examination. What is most likely, however," said he, "some dark night your boats would have been smashed to kindling-wood;

your stores, papers, and valuables would have been taken away, and yourselves turned adrift in a swamp."

"But," said I, "you don't mean to say that a great government would permit such a thing?"

"Oh, of course not! Our great government would express the most profound regret at the accident; it would insist that the damage was done not by police agents, but by common thieves. In any event, you would be stopped before you got a hundred miles away from St. Petersburg, and, what is more, you would never be able to prove that the government had stopped you.

"In Russia we are far ahead of Western Europe. We have copied lynch-law from America, only here the government does the lynching. When a man is obnoxious, reads or writes or talks too much, we do not bother about courts and sheriffs. He disappears—that is all. When his friends come to inquire after him, the government shrugs its shoulders, and knows nothing about it. He has been killed by robbers, perhaps, or he has committed suicide! The government cannot be held responsible for every traveller in Russia, of course!

"When a military attaché is suspected of knowing too much about Russian affairs, his rooms are always broken into and ransacked. Not by the government—oh dear, no! That would be shocking! It is always done by burglars. But, odd to say, these Russian burglars always care particularly for *papers and letters.*

"The German military attaché has had his rooms broken into twice in this manner, and to prevent a third invasion he assured the chief of police that there was no use doing it any more, that he really never kept any important papers there. Since then he has not been troubled by official burglars."

VI

We were turned out upon the platform at Kovno at a quarter-past four of a misty and chilly morning, and, after wandering about this mysterious fortress-town until its only population, Jews and soldiers, filled the streets, we embarked on a little steamboat bound down the Niemen. One of the passengers had answered my many questions in a friendly manner, and with him I had considerable talk about smugglers, Jews, Cossacks, and things in general. Two men in uniform on the opposite side of the boat watched us with strange intentness, and for that reason I took pains that our Russian friend should know that we were merely American tourists visiting his beautiful country in search of the picturesque.

He disappeared soon after the boat started,

and Remington curled himself up in the stern-sheets for the purpose of making studies of peasant costumes. He had not filled many pages before a hand was placed on my shoulder, and my Russian friend whispered in my ear,

"If you don't both of you wish to spend the next few days in jail, make your friend stop his note-making."

"But," I said, "he is not making notes; he is a famous American artist, filling his sketch-book with bits of costume."

And, to convince him of Remington's innocence, I showed him the book, full of memorandum sketches, which, however, seemed only to make our case worse.

"This is not a matter for joking," said he, earnestly. "Two officers on board are watching you. Every day some one disappears on suspicion of playing the spy. Only last week two women were locked up in the fortress overnight for having inadvertently strayed upon suspicious ground. They had come up the river with their husbands in a holiday party, and it was only with the greatest difficulty that they got clear again. The men who are watching you will make no distinction between sketching a peasant's nose and pacing off a fort front."

We thanked him for his disinterested advice, Remington promptly packed his book, and our friend was soon once more in conversation with

"'TWO OFFICERS ARE WATCHING YOU'"

the sour-looking officials, apparently convincing them that we were not worth locking up, being merely a couple of crazy American artists, with very scant baggage. Had it not been for the intercession of that intelligent young Russian, there is little doubt in my mind that we should have been arrested at the next landing, robbed of all our sketches and notes, taken back to Kovno, and kept in jail for a week or so, or until our chargé in St. Petersburg had discovered a diplomatic precedent which should justify him in demanding our release.

The two officers accompanied us to the last station in Russia, saw us safely off, and then returned to the nearest telegraph office to report that they had successfully driven two inquiring foreigners out of their country, and done it so neatly that no one could possibly take offence; no one could accuse the czar's government of breaking any rule of international courtesy!

As I pen these lines, a letter from our chargé in St. Petersburg reaches me confirming all that was told us there more than a month ago, namely, that the Russian government simply ignored his application, and by so doing gave him to understand that Remington should not make sketches in Russia, and that the United States deserved a snub for sending a commissioner to inquire about tree-planting on the sea-coasts.

In other words, the Russian government treated Remington and myself exactly as it treated the Emigration Commission sent by the United States government last year. When Japan declined to receive an American commissioner some forty years ago, we sent a fleet under Commodore Perry and insisted upon the forms of European courtesy. That was bullying a chivalrous but weak nation. To-day our diplomatic representatives in Russia are treated with the same contempt we have learned to expect in China, and latterly Chile.

## VII

A word about our precious canoes. These had been fitted with folding centre-boards and drop-rudders; had each two masts and sails; had water-tight compartments fore and aft; were admirably adapted for a long cruise, and floated the burgee of the New York Canoe Club. Our idea was to haul them ashore at night, hoist a specially fitted tent over each well, sleep on board, and, if necessary, cook our meals as well. Remington had invented a water-proof holder for his sketching material, exactly fitted to the canoe, and in both boats everything was done that could possibly add to the success of our cruise from St. Petersburg to Berlin.

C. B. Vaux, the author of the standard text-

A PAGE OF SKETCHES MADE ON THE NIEMEN

book for canoeists, gave us his advice, so did the veteran cruiser C. J. Stevens, the secretary of the club. The Hamburg-American Steamship Company triced the little squadron up under the boom over the after-deck, and allowed us this as a part of our personal baggage—a courtesy which we highly appreciated. From Hamburg the boats went to Lübeck by rail, about one hour and a half; thence by steamboat directly to

St. Petersburg. The whole cost per boat between Hamburg and St. Petersburg was 40 rubles, say $20, making about $10 apiece for the whole journey, including the transfers in Hamburg, Lübeck, and St. Petersburg. In parenthesis I might add that the freight charges in Germany are so low upon canoes as to make land carriage quite as cheap as water. Last year, for instance, my canoe was taken from the coast of Holland to the head-waters of the Danube by fast freight for 12.90 marks, about $3.20, at which rate I should have shipped my canoe back from St. Petersburg to Kovno for about $4.

Kovno is about fifty miles from the Prussian frontier, on a river called Niemen by the Russians, and Memel by Germans. It was for us the only way of getting to Tilsit without touching the Baltic coast first; and being on the direct railway line between St. Petersburg and Berlin, promised the greatest speed. The express trains make the distance in thirty hours, and the ordinary ones in forty-eight, the distance being about 550 miles. In order to have no possible mistake in regard to our retreat, we accepted the kind offices of a Russian friend connected with the Foreign Office. He took us to the proper express agency, explained in detail what was to be done, arranged that the boats should go off immediately by the fast freight travelling with the passenger train, had the bill made out for us, and stipulated that we should pay on receipt of the canoes.

We gave those canoes forty-eight hours' start, and found on arrival in Kovno that there was no record of them whatever. The chief of the station said he understood no French or German, but by the assistance of an intelligent young woman who operated the telegraph, we came to an understanding.

I showed him our passports and credentials, told him we expected our boats here, and asked him if he would forward them on to us when they came. He said he would.

We then asked if he wished payment on bill of lading. He said that was not necessary; the boats would be sent right on across the frontier as soon as they arrived, and the money collected at the other end.

I then left with the intelligent young telegraph operator our address, and money to defray cost of messages. She refused the money present we offered her—conclusive evidence that she was not Russian.

All this happened on June 10th. Remington and I meanwhile went down the river by steamer; made a few excursions to kill time; finally located ourselves at Trakehnen, about ten miles from the Russian frontier, only sixty miles from Kovno, and waited patiently for our canoes.

On June 11th came a Russian telegram which

to us was a muddle: "If wooden boats must pay in Kovno, if metal can be paid in Trakehnen."

A high German official, whose guests we were, happened to be an intimate personal friend of the German consul in Kovno, and therefore, to simplify the whole matter, he kindly telegraphed him to pay all charges, and do everything needful to hurry the boats on. We certainly thought that this would be guarantee enough for the Russian police.

On June 13th, when we expected to be far away in our boats down the Pregel, came another Kovno cable saying that 92 rubles must be paid before the railway chief would let the boats start. Of course we cabled back that money was no object, that the German consul was responsible, and that we wanted the boats very badly.

We waited another twenty-four hours, and then came another vexatious cable—that Kovno would not forward the boats until they had received the bill of lading. We were now indignant, because we had offered the bill of lading once before, and it had been declined; and, besides, the German consul surely was guarantee enough that we were not tramps. At last, on the 16th, came a cable from the German consul saying that the bill of lading had come, and that the charges against us amounted to 100 rubles, or 300 marks, say $70,

or about double what they should h.
We cabled back to pay up and send the bc

We had long ago made up our minds that
Russians in Kovno were doing their best to spo.
our canoe cruise by obstructions of the most un-
necessary kind.

At last, after an infinite amount of worry and
needless expense, the canoes reached Stettin, on
the Baltic, on the 2d of July, having been on the
way since the 8th of June.

At Kovno the police were curious to know
what was in the boat of Remington, so they took
a hammer and smashed a hole through the beautiful mahogany deck, in spite of the fact that the
hatches were on purpose left unlocked.

Remington waited about Europe for a whole
month, hoping from day to day that our diplomatic representative in St. Petersburg would secure, at least for him, the necessary police permit to make sketches.* He has gone home now,
and left me to write the net results of this mem-
orable railway canoe cruise—a wasted month, an
empty pocket, a smashed canoe.

* It is proper here to say that after a delay of two months, and when it was no longer of use, the formal permit was accorded to both the author and artist by the Russian authorities.

## THE RUSSIAN AND HIS JEW

RUSSIA has more than a third of all the Jews in the world, and she is doing her best to reduce this number. Official statistics are not quite reliable on this subject, but it is assumed by the best-informed that Russia must have close on to 3,000,000 of the Hebrew race. The United States and England are shocked by the measures which the czar is taking against these people, and charge him with reviving religious persecution. The czar replies to this by pointing out that the United States deliberately closed its doors against emigration from China, whose subjects were represented in America to the extent of only about 100,000 souls, mostly upon the Pacific coast. In this matter, moreover, the czar moves in harmony with the overwhelming majority of his people, high and low; and were his people to-morrow to proclaim a republic, one of the few laws which it would not repeal would be that which excludes the Jew from Holy Russia. The Russian knows his Jew better than we know him, and is therefore better qualified to legislate on the subject.

The general outburst of indignation which greeted the anti-Jewish legislation of Russia since the accession of the present czar may be accounted for in many ways. The newspapers and banks of Europe are largely in Jewish hands, and this power was of course quickly evoked to create public sympathy for their persecuted co-religionists. The popular sentiment was, however, most intelligent and most effective in the countries immediately bordering upon Russia, whose people wasted little time in theorizing on the rights of man or the beauties of tolerance, but organized with a view of protecting themselves against an influx of unwelcome immigrants. Castle Garden is not the only point to which the Jew of Russia has fled for comfort. He is equally keen in his desire to find a home in western Europe, where he can live in towns, pursue his life as broker, and not be too far away from the headquarters of his religious inspiration. America, England, France, Spain, Italy, Holland, Sweden, Norway—these countries have few Jews, comparatively speaking, and they are pretty well distributed. The stranger walking down Broadway, guided by the signs over the shops of jobbers and importers, might conclude that the Jews own New York, yet what we have is a mere nothing to what one country of Russia alone — Poland — has, whose Jewish population, according to the last census, was about 800,000. In England, Jews are met in every walk of life—in the army, the diplomatic service, the cabinet, the House of Lords, and amongst the boon companions of England's future king. As with us, they have cast off every distinguishing badge of their race, and it is frequently only by accident that we learn the nature of their religious creed. In Russia, however, it is totally different. There the Jew is as distinct a type as is with us the negro or the Chinaman. You can distinguish him as far as you can see, not merely by the face and form, so graphically drawn by Mr. Pennell in his work *The Jew at Home*, but in certain peculiarities of dress, to which he clings as pertinaciously as does the Apache to his blanket or the Mexican to his sombrero. The Jew of Kovno, Warsaw, Kiev, and wherever else I have run across him in Russia, wears a curious curl that hangs down in front of each ear, sometimes to his chin. His cap of black alpaca or cloth sits far back on his head, close to his ears, with a visor as large as those once fashionable amongst our brakemen and conductors. His coat of black cloth or alpaca is modelled after that in which Dundreary is usually portrayed, reaching down to his ankles, and assisting to give him the long, lean, hungry look of the Shylock type. On his feet are boots worn outside of his trousers, in one hand an umbrella, in the other a valise; for the Jew in Russia is usually moving from place to place on business, unless he is so poor as to be forced into menial occupation.

A Russian who is not a Jew-hater by any means, but a thoroughly practical man of affairs, told me that next to the Jew's love of money was his devotion to the Talmud and its expounders. Strange as it may seem to us, who think of the Jew as wandering into all the corners of the world, guided solely by the desire of making money, we find that, on the contrary, he is fastened to Russia by the holiest of ties, that he wears his peculiar dress as proudly as a Highlander does his kilt, and that he does everything in his power to remain at home and discourage others from leaving. To draw the orthodox Jew educated in the school of the Talmud, away from the centre of his religious education, if not inspiration, is to him a serious matter.

We propose to place before the inquiring reader a short sketch of the manner in which the Jew is regarded to-day by those who dread his westward migration, and to bring together some of the reasons put forward by those who are so illiberal as to dislike his company. Russia has limited the territory in which Jews are allowed to live to a narrow strip, beginning in the Baltic provinces near Riga, and ending at the Black Sea, following, roughly, the western frontier of the empire, along the borders of Prussia, Austria, Hungary, and Roumania. These four countries—or rather three, if we regard Austria and Hungary as one—know more of the Jews by actual contact than any other people; for, according to the last census on the subject, there were in Austro-Hungary 1,643,708; German Empire, 567,884; Roumania, 400,000.

The same census gave for Great Britain and Ireland only 46,000 Jews; France, 49,439; Norway, only 34; Spain, 402—in fact, as compared with Russia's neighbors, the number of Jews in other countries is hardly worth mentioning.

The Chinese question in America was settled with reference purely to the Chinaman as he was known in California, and did not take into consideration the best class of Chinese in their own country. The Russian regards the Jew from his standpoint as it affects himself personally, and not from the standpoint of an Englishman or an

American, who has in view Jews of a nobler type. The Jew of Russia shades off into the Polish Jew, then into the German Jew, and it is a mixture of these two that is now besieging Castle Garden for American citizenship. How many Jews emigrate from Russia every year is not known, for large numbers smuggle themselves over the frontier, and are most difficult to identify, because of the similarity in feature and dress of all the Chosen People along this Jewish strip. When I was in Kovno I came in contact with a Jew who told me that his whole business in life was smuggling his co-religionists out of the country at a fixed price per head.

The present alleged persecution of the Jews in Russia consists not so much in the making of offensive regulations against them as in enforcing laws of long standing, which the Jews have evaded by the assistance of the police, and of course by heavy bribes. The law has distinctly prohibited Jews in general from settling in Russia proper, exception being made only in certain cases, covering artists, scholars, physicians, and specially privileged merchants. But so clever were the Jews in manipulating the officials, or, perhaps it is equally true to say, so greedy were the officials for an addition to their scanty salary, that in all the towns of Russia proper Jews had notoriously congregated who were theoretically outlaws. Moscow and St. Petersburg, for instance, had each as many as 40,000 contrabands of this description. The Jews must have been a source of great profit to the officials, or they would not have been so long tolerated; and, on the other hand, there must have been large opportunities for making money, or this race would not have exposed itself to so many dangers and sacrifices by placing itself in a position to be periodically raided by the police. That the Jews are now being forced to conform to the law of Russia is an indication not merely that the government has awakened to a sense of its legal duties, but that the financial burdens laid upon the Jews in Russia are greater than they are willing to bear; in other words, they are too poor to purchase the immunity of former years.

"Why do you hate the Jew?" I one day asked my Russian friend.

"Because," said he, "the Jew brings nothing into the country, he takes all he can out of it, and while he is here he makes the peasant his slave, and lives only for the sake of squeezing money out of everything."

This was a strong statement, but he went on to amplify it by a variety of illustrations.

After the Polish insurrection of 1863, the Russian government set to work energetically to russify that country, and particularly Lithuania. The principal means they employed, aside from actively persecuting the heterodox in religion

JEWS AT A PEASANT MARKET

and politics, was to colonize large numbers of peasants from the interior of Russia upon farms which had been confiscated. Agricultural implements were furnished to these peasants, and everything was done to start them well, so as to form a nucleus of Russian life in the midst of the disloyal provinces. Twenty years have passed since this great russifying measure was put into force, and what is the result?

If, as a traveller, you come into a Russian village, it is dirtier, if possible, than those of the neighboring Lithuanians and Poles. You ask for horses to continue your journey, and are quickly supplied by these Russians; the price is fixed, and you are about to pay it to the Russian who brings your carriage to the door. He, however, refuses to take it, and begs that you will pay the money not to him, but to the proprietor of the tavern. You ask why. He answers that he is not allowed to take any money, that the horses he has brought belong to the Jew. You begin to inquire, and you find that the Jew not only owns the tavern, but trades in all the articles which the peasants have to buy. You learn also that the Jew is creditor to nearly every peasant for miles around, and has a lien upon everything which that peasant may grow upon his land. You find that the peasant cultivates his land not for himself, but for the Jew, and that all his reward is the privilege of bare existence.

There are many patriotic and humane Russians who have given it to me as their deliberate opinion that the Russian peasant would be better off to-day had he never been emancipated. He is dreamy, good-natured, unpractical, and very ignorant. When he is hard pressed for money, it is only too easy for him to accept the loan which the accommodating tavern-keeper offers him, particularly if he has one or two glasses of vodka inside of him. Like a child, he thinks little of the ultimate consequences and much of the present enjoyment. He signs the paper which is placed before him, and believes, of course, that he will easily pay off his debt with the next harvest, particularly as the Jew promises to be most accommodating, and not press for money payment. He sends, of course, the produce of his farm to the Jew, who acts as broker for him, and reserves his commission, and what he is pleased to consider the interest on his money; and by some mysterious method of calculation the peasant is always the debtor, and the Jew always happy to accommodate him still further on the same terms.

As my Russian friend explained the situation, it reminded me forcibly of several statements of the same kind made to me in Georgia and Alabama a few years ago, where I visited some friends, who knew the condition of their communities very well, and were in no sense Jew-haters. There I was told that the freedom which the Northern States had purchased for the negro at the cost of so much blood and treasure had been since sold to the Jew. The same Jews who had learned to play upon human nature by intercourse with emancipated serfs found in the Southern States exactly the material best suited for their purposes.

The Jew opens a general country store, and bends all his energies towards making himself agreeable to the negroes by letting them have whatever they choose without paying for it. In this manner an account soon runs up, in regard to which the negro is rarely prudent enough to keep an exact tally. When it has reached a proper figure, the Jew presses for payment, and of course the negro has no money. But the Jew assures the negro that nothing is further from his purpose than to do anything that might seem greedy. He waives the question of money entirely, and asks only that the negro pay him in cotton, or perhaps by handing over a mule or a cow, and by promising to continue trading at his store. This seems very magnanimous to the negro, and he cheerfully signs away future crops, to say nothing of the very farm he is working. Thus the negro works from year to year, always tied to the soil by the debt he owes the Jew, and as little capable of independent action as he or his ancestors ever were before 1863.

In the Southern States, as in Russia, the liberal stranger naturally asks, "Why do not the peasants themselves, or the negroes, organize their own shops, and thus protect themselves against extortion and practical slavery?" It is a question easily asked, but the actual fact is that they do not, and that in both Russia and the United States blacks and peasants are bound to the soil by a slavery that is more galling than that they were formerly subjected to, because they are mocked with the title of free men.

It was not until after the emancipation of the serfs, in 1861, that the Jew question began to take on serious proportions; for up to that time the peasant had, in his landlord, a protector who was able to shield him from the consequences of his improvidence. After the emancipation, however, the gulf between peasant and proprietor became as wide as that which separated the black from his former master; and between these two classes there entered an army of Jews, who alone have profited by the edict of 1861. The peasants became easy victims, owing to their improvidence and love of drink; but the proprietors soon found that they could accomplish nothing without the assistance of the money-lender, and, above all, the only man who could control the labor market. Jews were, to be sure, not allowed to acquire real estate, but in the western provinces they took charge of landed property as agents

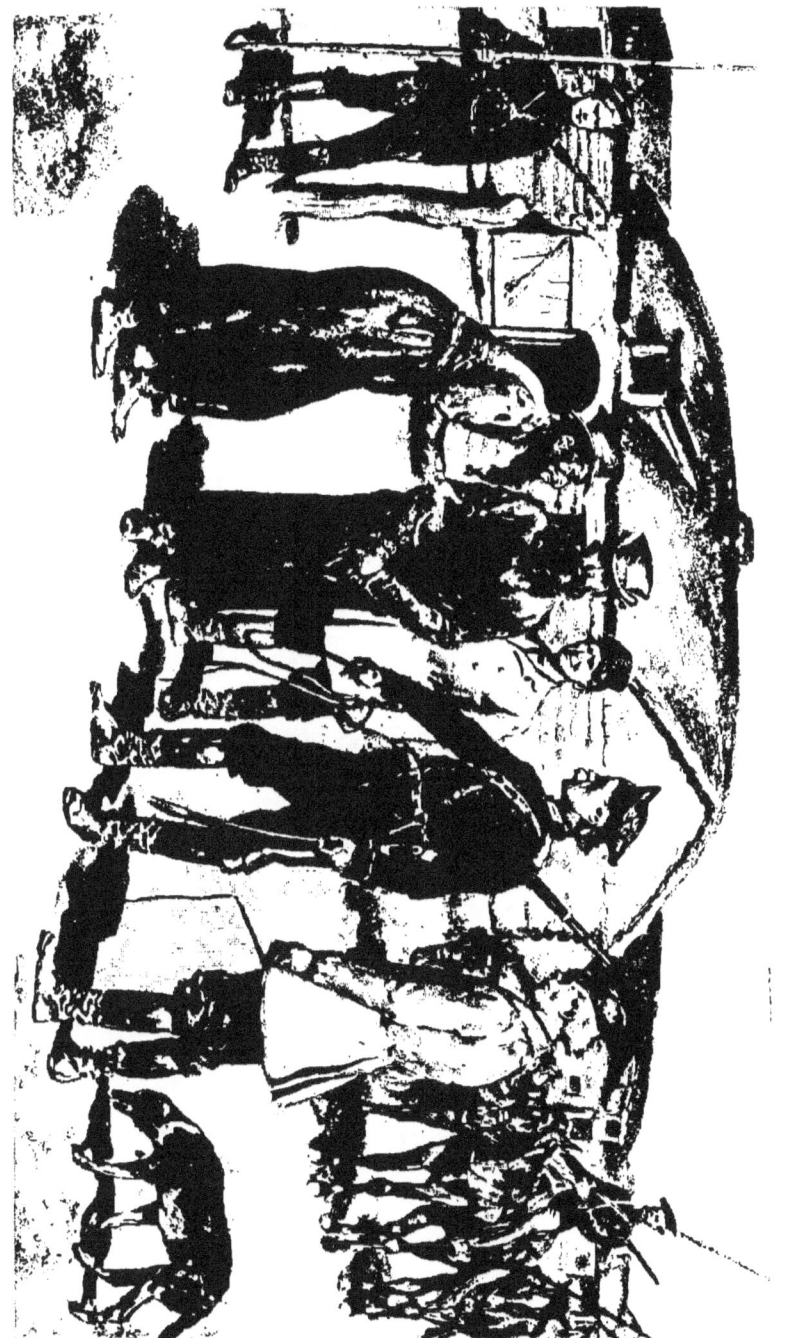

in such a manner that they had all the substantial benefits of ownership with none of the drawbacks. All the supplies for the estate were bought of themselves and charged to the unlucky proprietor; by their hold upon the peasants they were able to enforce labor at nominal rates, and nothing prevented them from exhausting the soil as rapidly as possible, cutting down all the timber, and when they had squeezed the last kopeck out of the property, moving off to some other estate and commencing the same process over again. It is to the multiplicity of such cases that we must refer some of the present distress in Russia, although, of course, many other reasons co-operate. I am informed on good authority that, in spite of laws to the contrary, a very large proportion of the land within the pale is practically in Jewish hands, to say nothing of the peasants who work upon it. To how great an extent this is the case is as difficult to find out as to give the exact number of Jews in Russia, for they have a direct interest in deceiving the government in regard to both of these matters, and have, so far, succeeded very well.

A witty German once said, sneeringly, of the Russians, that "every nation is afflicted with the sort of Jew best suited to its condition;" but if this is true, it is the most damning verdict upon the Poles, whose Jews appear to be upon the lowest level of human existence which it has been my fortune to meet with. This aphorism might be paraphrased by saying that each country has the Chinaman best suited for it, and that therefore California should have been content with her contingent from the Flowery Kingdom.

The public sentiment of Europe—at least, the eastern portion of it—might have been measured in the Berlin conference after the Russo-Turkish war, when Lord Beaconsfield made his notable effort in favor of the Jews. His proposals did not fall upon sympathetic ears, and the utmost he accomplished was to cause the powers to bully Roumania into a formal recognition of the Jews as equal in citizenship with the rest of the people. But even in Roumania the law is almost a dead letter by reason of a series of regulations subsequently passed. The Roumanian to-day dreads an increase of his Jewish population almost as much as an invasion of Russian troops, and if the papers of his country cry out against Russian intolerance, it is not because he sympathizes with the Jews, but because he fears lest further persecution in Russia will make it more difficult for him to keep them out of Roumania.

Germany and Austria can look on with something like equanimity while isolated Jews filter across the frontiers and merge into the rest of the population. They still maintain a pose of tolerance to all creeds, but it would be hazardous to say how long this attitude can be safely maintained. Russia has not yet given the signal, but it is not beyond the realm of probability to imagine religious fanaticism so harmonizing with popular hatred as to produce a law not simply confining the Jews to Russian provinces on the western frontier, but actually expelling them by thousands and hundreds of thousands out of the country. Could Germany and Austria look with equanimity upon such an immigration into their already crowded countries? Or, aside from governmental action, can we suppose that the people of these countries would endure such a Jewish movement with any more kindliness than was manifested in San Francisco towards the cargoes of Chinamen? Germany and Austria know that Russia has an almost inexhaustible supply of this undesirable population, all living along a single strip of territory, and united by centuries of common language, traditions, and family ties to such a degree as to make them a state within a state, as much so as the Mormon Church. Up to within recent years the Jewish communities have been allowed to govern themselves according to their own peculiar laws and customs, much as the Chinese manage their own affairs in Chinatown. These peculiar privileges are now abolished, but custom and tradition amongst them, notably their religious preceptors, have so complete an ascendency over them that the effect of the Russian law upon them does not go far beyond the presence of the policeman.

My Russian friend, who had given considerable attention to the history of the Jews, as well as to their present condition in Russia, called my attention to the great difference between the Jew of Russia—that is to say, the Jew who calls into existence the anti-Semitic movement in Germany —and his co-religionist who was driven out of Spain about the time that Columbus discovered America. The Jews of Spain, whom Ferdinand and Isabella expelled from the country, stood upon a relatively high plane of intellectual as well as material development. In that age of monkish superstition the Jews stood forth preeminent as masters in many sciences. They had enjoyed successive generations of contact with highly refined people, had absorbed the artistic spirit, which no one could escape who lived in the Spain of that time. The short-sighted fanaticism which drove them out into the world called forth much sympathy for them; and the fame of their learning, particularly in the natural sciences, did much to atone for the prejudice against their money-making propensities. Then, too, these Spanish refugees did not all move to one country, nor did they come from a land that might furnish additional supplies in the future. The Jews of 1492 scattered themselves broadcast into nearly every country of western Europe, notably

Italy, England, Holland, South Germany, and France. The Popes of Rome extended their protection to them, and, in spite of occasional outbursts of popular ill-will, they prospered, and with their prosperity gradually took on the color of the society in which they moved, and lost correspondingly the peculiar characteristics which are so conspicuous in the Russian Jew. The Jews of four hundred years ago, who wandered in distress to Antwerp, London, Amsterdam, Naples, Venice, Marseilles, Genoa, Rome, brought to all these cities talents which the people there knew how to appreciate. Their appearance there might almost be compared to that of the clever artisans and manufacturers who came to England and Prussia after the Revocation of the Edict of Nantes—in the sense that the best people of the country regarded them as a source of economic strength. But the Jew who to-day comes from the Russian border to Berlin or Buda-Pesth represents in no sense a man of learning, or even the master of an art whose acquisition is envied by the people amongst whom he settles. He represents to them unscrupulous greed for money, a marvellous facility in deception—a man whose object in life seems to be to subordinate every consideration to that of material success. All England has only about as many Jews as the capital of Prussia alone, and the Jew question as it appears to the German is intensified by the reflection that the Jew who comes to him from the East is not only a creature repugnant to him individually, but who has left behind him so vast a number of his co-religionists that if they once start upon an invasion of western Europe they will soon be in a position to dictate terms in every Christian capital. The Spanish Jew and the Russian Jew are, of course, allied, if we go back far enough; but no Russian or German finds any comfort in reflecting upon the excellence of the Jews in the days of Columbus. His apprehension springs entirely from observing the Jew of to-day.

Said my friend to me: "Wherever the Jew has control of the press—and that is saying a good deal—you find that he strenuously preaches tolerance, in order that he may profit by it. To read the articles by Jews in newspapers and reviews, one would suppose that the only truly liberal spirits to-day were the members of synagogues. If you will take my word for it—and I think I know what I am talking about—there is no church domination that can be more narrow and relentless than that which governs the four or five millions of Jews who occupy both sides of the Russian frontier between the Baltic and the Black Sea."

In 1877 a Jewess named Ida Katzhandel chose to turn Roman Catholic and marry a Pole. The pair lived happily for about a year, when one fine

JEWISH SMUGGLERS AND REFUGEES IN THE HANDS OF THE DRAGOONS

day the relations of Ida turned up while the husband was away, took her from the house, and drowned her in the river Wieprz—a stream which runs into the Vistula near Ivan-Gorod. The guilty ones had taken, of course, every precaution against discovery; but the police managed, somehow or other, to trace the crime home, and the murderers were brought to trial in Lublin about three years after the murder. Two of them were convicted; one was sentenced to two years' penal servitude, the other to two years' confinement; with regard to the remainder the evidence was so faulty that they had to be set free, although there was no doubt in the minds of the people in the neighborhood as to who had committed this outrage. But stranger than the crime was the fact that during the days of this trial the space about the court-house was filled with violent Jews, who praised the murderers as martyrs to their religion, and who greeted those who had been released as men to whom every honor was due.

My Russian friend assured me that the picture of brutal fanaticism furnished by this one instance is typical of the great mass of Jews whom the German has in mind, as well as the Russian, when he discusses the Jew question. One can scarcely conceive of grosser religious intolerance than this in Spain of 1492 or Mexico of 1892. It is a picture for which, I confess, I was little prepared, and it is obvious that the Jew of Lublin has but a distant blood-relation with those who produced a philosopher like Spinoza.

Russians have told me that it is almost impossible to catch the Jews for military service, owing to the facilities they enjoy of changing their domicile. The railways have been in Russia the greatest possible blessing to the Jews, in that they give them the means of speedily moving from place to place, transacting business in parts of the country where they are forbidden, and disappearing with their profits to a place of safety before the government has become aware of what has happened. Forged passports are readily procured, and with these they move from point to point, sleeping on the train, and transacting their business through the day. They avoid as much as possible spending any time in a town where they might be called to account by the police. When the recruiting authorities come to hunt up their Jews for the military service which all Russians have to render, they are usually away from home, or have been enrolled in some other town or village. If they are finally caught and brought before the military authorities, they usually have papers certifying that they are either too young or too old for the service; in fact, the military authorities regard it now as pretty well proved that of the three million Jews in the Russian Empire, hardly one is of military age. In this matter of deceiving the War Office the Jews are much assisted by their local Jewish officials, whose duty it is to register births and grant certificates of this kind ; but the matter at last went to such ridiculous lengths that the Russians have gone to the other extreme, and now attach no importance whatever to any document which the Jew may produce, but draw their own conclusions by looking at him, and pronounce him of military age or not according to his appearance or their inclinations. I ventured to point out to my friend that there was little inducement for the Jew to enter the army, where he was not apt to be treated with much consideration, but my friend replied that the behavior of the Jew in regard to his military service was analogous to his behavior in regard to all his obligations to the state and every community except his own.

"I do not know how it is with you in America," said he, "but with us, whenever you see a Jew who is rich, you may be pretty sure that he has either contracted to furnish food or clothing for the army, or else has been several times bankrupt. You would have great difficulty in discovering a rich Jew who has not been bankrupt at least once."

The attitude of Germans towards Jews is necessarily most intimately connected with the treatment of them by the czar, which illustrates, what I believe to be the fact, that the Germans who discuss this question without religious bitterness are prepared to treat fairly the Jews now in Germany, but dread the political consequences of a further immigration from the east. It is notable that the anti-Semitic movement sprang into existence in Germany at the same time that Alexander III. became czar, and has been growing in proportion as that sovereign has shown a disposition to rid himself of them at the expense of his western neighbors. Fair-minded Germans have over and over again repudiated the idea that they could object to Jews, or any one else, on religious grounds, and protested that in approaching this question they did so strictly as practical politicians dealing with a political state of things gravely affecting the future of their country's development. They do not dread a Jewish invasion from the west, for that Jew is no longer the Jew of Poland, but the Jew who has conformed in many ways to the life and thought of his neighbors in Holland, Belgium, England, and France. The Jew question in Germany could be easily settled if England would agree to accept them first after they left Poland, and send them on to Germany only after they had spent a generation on her soil, far from the influences that oppress them in Warsaw and Kovno.

That the Jew question in Germany has reference to fears for the future rather than anxiety

JEWISH RECRUITS

in regard to the present is illustrated to some extent by the fact that in Germany all religious denominations are treated as equal before the law, and if a Jew in Germany complains that his position in society is not as desirable as he could wish, it is a complaint that might just as well be made in America, or even in England. The German Jew complains that his co-religionists are not often selected for military commands, and argues that he is therefore not equal before the law. The Jew is not often found as an officer in the German army simply because the majority of German officers do not desire to serve with him. If the officers of a Prussian regiment desired a Jew to become one of their number, there is no law in the country that would stand in the way; for in this matter of becoming an officer the Jew stands on a footing as good as and no better than a Christian. Every candidate for epaulets in the German army submits his name to the regiment in which he desires to serve, and has to be elected into the regiment, much as though he were applying for admission into a rowing club, or any other semi-social organization. The present German custom is an excellent one, and the Jews who complain against it only advertise the fact that they have not yet reached a point where their fellow-countrymen regard them as the most desirable leaders of troops.

Germany, with a population less than fifty millions, has, according to the census of 1890, 567,884 Jews, a trifle over one per cent. of the population, and a larger number than the whole of her standing army. Of this number Prussia alone has 372,058, yet nowhere have the Jews more enlightened champions than amongst Germans who are not even of the Jewish faith, notably the editors of such papers as the *Nation* and the *Freisinnige*, both of whom are active members of the German Parliament. These men and the party they represent scout the idea that so small a proportion of the whole population can possibly become a danger, and they loudly urge the government to appoint Jews to the most important military and judicial posts — in other words, to treat a Jew not as an alien, but as a thorough German. But these statesmen have not yet convinced the great mass of the people that the Jew, by becoming a citizen of the German Empire, necessarily becomes a German other than in name and speech. Prussia, in 1850, made her citizenship equal to all, irrespective of religious denomination, and has treated the Jew substantially as the Christian, at least before the law, and the Imperial Constitution of 1871 was framed in the same spirit of toleration.

German politicians who to-day champion the cause of the Jews tell us that during the wars of liberation against Napoleon I. five and a half per cent. of the Jews who were of the military age entered the Prussian army as volunteers, and that one of the first soldiers to earn the Iron Cross in those wars was a Jew. From that day to this the Jews in Germany have borne a good record in the ranks of the army, although few of them have become officers.

Dr. Phillippson has raised a monument to German Jews in connection with the war of 1870 by publishing the result of investigations made among his co-religionists in 132 communities. His conclusions are that the Jewish population furnished its full complement to the active army during that struggle, and earned a very respectable number of Iron Crosses as the reward of bravery. The Jews have warm friends in Germany, both in Parliament and in the press, and the merits of the Jew question are pretty thoroughly discussed there from every point of view. In no community is religious toleration so much a matter of principle as in Germany, and the idea of making a distinction between Jew and Christian on religious grounds never entered the mind of a practical German legislator. Every German school-boy is brought up to regard the greatness of Prussia as owing largely to the refuge it has afforded in past ages to the persecuted of all other countries, whether Protestants from France or Jews from Spain. But even amongst liberal Germans there is growing up a feeling that the Jews of their country are more than their mere numbers represent; that they are to some extent a political society whose organization covers the world, and whose aims are not altogether those of the citizens amongst whom they are protected. No Protestant German has ill-will towards his fellow-citizen of the Roman Catholic faith, and if Lutherans ever show a disposition to depart from their principle of toleration it is when they have reason to dread the influence of Jesuits as a political power, whose centre is not within the limits of the empire. The Jewish question is growing in importance amongst Germans, as it has grown in importance in Hungary, in Roumania, and, above all, in Russia. It is bound to go on increasing in proportion as the Jews decline to identify themselves completely with the people amongst whom they traffic and make their money. It is not a trifling matter that the people of these countries regard the Israelite as one of a different nation and race, but it is vastly more serious when amongst these people there develops a widespread fear that the supply of Jews from Russia may assume proportions still more disastrous.

## SIDE LIGHTS ON THE GERMAN SOLDIER

MY friend Captain Zinnowitz came to dinner with me one night in Berlin. He was invited particularly to meet Remington, and we spent a long evening together talking about his work as an officer of the Prussian army. I knew that he had been into Russian Poland several times for the benefit of his government, and therefore drew the conversation on to the best means of succeeding at this delicate work.

"When I go into Poland," said he, "I am not an officer any longer; I dress my hair differently, and become simply plain Mr. ——, who is seeking employment as a hydraulic engineer. I have, of course, an address in a small provincial German town, from which all my letters come and where

I have a trusted friend ready to answer all questions in regard to my occupation and identity should the Russian secret police make inquiries in regard to me. Last year I was instructed to report upon a line of railway projected at a certain point in Poland, and for that reason hired a Jew to pilot me. We went together for some distance, when the Jew told me that there were two policemen on the train evidently on our tracks, and that he would go no farther. I went on alone, and at the next station jumped off on the side farthest from the railway station, and made for the woods. I had not gone far, however, when the two policemen overtook me, and demanded to know what my business was. Of course I had to make up a plausible story, and therefore remarked that I was buying wood, and had to inspect the forests of the neighborhood. Upon this, one of them said that there were no forests in the direction in which I was going, and that I must accompany them to the police station. To this I objected, protesting that I had been informed of a vast amount of timber cut and stored near here. Now this timber had all been cut for the purposes of the railway I was to report upon. The Russian policemen admitted that such was the case, much to my satisfaction, but said that they must take me to headquarters, under any circumstances, where I would be examined as a matter of form. So off we went to-

DRAGOON OFFICER IN STREET DRESS

gether, the policemen leading me into the very fort that I did not dream of getting into, because it was a new one, guarded with particular jealousy, and one about which my government was very anxious to gain accurate information. As we marched along, however, the question of how to get rid of my secret notes embarrassed me, for had anything of this kind been found upon me, of course I should have been taken out and hanged. To accomplish my object I pulled out cigars, which I offered to my guardians; they accepted them with an ill grace, but did not smoke them. As I proceeded to light mine, I held with the cigar a bit of the tissue-paper on which I had made memoranda, and as my match burned it lit not only my cigar, but consumed the tissue-paper I held in the hollow of my hand. I had to allow my cigar to go out several times in order to get rid of the notes I had made, and heaved a great sigh of relief when the last piece was destroyed. When we reached the fortress I was taken to the commandant and inspected carefully; that is to say, every part of my person was investigated to see if I had not concealed the smallest scrap of paper. My passport was then copied out, and I was allowed to go. They ordered me back the same way, but, by dint of very energetic language, I succeeded in persuading them to let me pass on to the next town, by which means I was enabled to go completely through the works of the fort, and report exactly upon their extent. On arrival home, after several more episodes of the same kind, my government suggested to me the desirability of knowing more of the interior construction of this work, and when I see you next year I will tell you some more."

Neither Remington nor I ever saw him again. He spoke of his adventures as lightly as though he were recounting some steeple-chase episode, and regarded quite as naturally that he should run the risk of being hanged from day to day as that he should wear his uniform and go to parade. A few months after this little dinner I dined with another interesting character, a young army surgeon with whom I had long had friendly relations. He appeared rather depressed, at first reluctant to answer my questions, but finally told me this:

"I have just come from Thorn, a fortress of Prussia on the Vistula, close to the Russian frontier. Last night I held the hand of a man who died in a semi-delirious state. He had crawled across the frontier with great difficulty, for he was in the last stages of disease, and had been brought down the river to this fortress to the military hospital. He gave a name that is not in the army list, and died without our being able to make out very much about him. I presume that now the authorities have discovered what they

**CUIRASSIER**
From a Sketch in Unter den Linden

wish; but I was forced to leave him immediately after his death. The night before he died he managed, with great difficulty, to let me know this much: He was an officer in the Prussian army, had disguised himself as a Lithuanian peasant, and had sought employment in the neighborhood of a fortress in Poland. For this purpose he had to make himself as dirty and ragged as the peasants about him, and to harden his hands and features so that he might not arouse the suspicion of his employers. He lived in a peasant's hut, and after several weeks succeeded in being employed to carry wood into the fortress. Little by little he succeeded in gaining the information he desired, partly by pacing off distances, partly by personal inspection, and partly by careful questioning of his fellow-workmen. The nervous exhaustion which followed this painful kind of work—laboring with his hands all day, and then using the night hours for his scientific work, combined with the hourly fear of detection — produced a state of body and mind which ended in a fever. The notes he had made were too valuable to be abandoned, so he determined, cost what it might, to get into Germany before he died. He just managed to succeed. The Prussian Intelligence Department has now complete knowledge on one point at least, and another officer has died happy in the consciousness of having done his duty."

This little anecdote is one of hundreds illustrating the difficulties in the way of keeping up what the Germans consider the Intelligence Department, or the Great General Staff of their army. Every German officer knows that if he wishes a furlough for six months, he can always get it accorded provided he gives his superiors the assurance that he means to employ his time not in seeking pleasure, but in gathering information valuable to his country; he may wish to learn a new language, to make a report upon a particular equipment of a particular foreign army, to study horse-breeding. No matter what it is, inquiry of every kind is encouraged, provided it bears directly or indirectly upon the efficiency of the service.

To illustrate the care taken of the soldier in the German army, let me mention the subject of shoes. There is in Berlin, in a very out-of-the-way place, a government museum devoted entirely to hygiene. The famous Professor Koch is the head of this excellent institution, or at least he was so when I last visited it. Among the exhibits the most interesting to me was a lot of boots and shoes, with explanatory legends in regard to the relative merit of them for marching purposes. The ones that appear to have given the greatest satisfaction were very broad in the toes; in fact, so broad that the foot appeared to have no support except upon the

A HEAVY SWELL—GUARD HUSSAR

sole, thus allowing the greatest possible room for the expansion of the bones. In lieu of stockings, the article recommended was a woollen rag cut square and folded over the foot according to the taste of the wearer. The great advantage of these square woollen rags over the stocking is that while the stocking is apt to wear a hole either at the heel or at the toe, this woollen rag is shifted every time the boot is taken off, and thus insures an equal distribution of friction over all its parts. When the woollen rag is taken off it is very easily washed, and dries much more readily than the stocking; it is also more conveniently folded in the knapsack, and perhaps even on the score of economy has something in its favor. Between this excellent woollen rag and the care taken in regard to the selection of boots and shoes, so much has been achieved for the foot-gear of the soldier that it has now become axiomatic that any difficulty with a soldier's feet must be presumed to spring from a soldier's own carelessness. There are two things which the German officer does not and cannot condone — one is non-efficiency of the soldier's rifle, the other a chafed foot. If either of these two takes place on the march or during the manœuvres, the soldier is immediately punished with arrest, and is not allowed to offer any excuse. During the different manœuvres of German army corps that I have attended, I can recall but a few cases of foot-sore men in the course of a day's work, and yet at all these field operations forced marches are a feature, in order to test the endurance of officers and men. The secret of this uniform excellence, as regards marching powers, lies in the training which the men receive. When they enter their company as recruits in October, the first thing that is impressed upon their minds is the importance of the shoe and the musket. No pains are spared in giving the men at the start comfortable foot-gear, and they are expected to look after this with as much interest as if it were a chronometer. In the spring following, when the snow is off the ground, marches are undertaken, and these are regulated as carefully as are the strokes and the courses of the college crew under the hands of the trainer. Each day the men march half a mile or so farther than the day before; each day they carry on their back an ounce or two more; each day the speed they are able to maintain is carefully noted; in fact, the record of a company's marching from day to day, until late into the summer, when they move into the open country, is kept as minutely as if it were a single picked company training for a match or competitive drill. The German soldier is educated and trained for the purpose of fighting, and to have a man fall out before he reaches the fire-line is looked upon as quite as much

a disaster as if he had been shot and wounded by the enemy. The art of war, as practised in Germany, is very much the art of "getting there," and it is the general who posts himself most advantageously at the critical moment that may be assumed to have won the battle. The marching of German troops is something quite extraordinary, not in the performance of any individual man or company or regiment, but in the fact that the commander-in-chief can count upon all the parts of his command accomplishing a very high average of collective work, each part doing substantially as much as the other.

The so-called "iron ration" is an institution to which the Germans attach great importance. It is the soldier's food in a preserved shape, and not to be opened except in an extreme case of necessity; as, for instance, on a forced march preceding a battle. In ordinary times he must forage and requisition as well as he can, but the iron ration must not be touched, no matter how weary he is after his day's march. The preparation of this iron ration has been the subject of extensive chemical investigation in Germany, in order to arrive at the article which concentrates the greatest amount of nutrition in the most enduring shape; the factories where this iron ration is prepared are not open to public inspection, although I have no doubt that the French have full information on this subject.

The Germans are very thrifty in their habits, and no one visiting a German barrack-room would suspect their military authorities of extravagance, yet in regard to uniforms they seem to us extremely liberal; each soldier has five uniforms for varying degrees of work. The most inexpensive is the coarse linen one used in summer about the barracks, and the most valuable one is that which he wears on extraordinary festive occasions, as, for instance, the grand review of the Guards in the spring of the year; but beyond all those which he wears at more or less frequent intervals is the uniform which he puts on when the Emperor issues his order to mobilize for war. Then is taken out the absolutely new uniform, and with this he marches to the front. The troops that marched to the frontier in 1870 looked as though ready for a review rather than for the dirty work of campaigning.

There is a tyranny amongst German officers which would strike us as outrageous—not tyranny over soldiers, but tyranny of superior officers over inferior ones. It can only be explained by the rules governing the admission of officers to the German army. In most countries, as with us, admission to the army is gained by passing stiff examinations and nothing more. In the German army, not only must a series of difficult examinations be passed, but the candidate for epaulets must at the same time be chosen into a regi-

THE OLD GENERAL

ment by the officers of that regiment. Thus a young man who may have shown his proficiency in military science may yet fail to become an officer if he is regarded as a disagreeable messfellow by every regiment in the army. Perhaps it is possible to plead that any man who cannot get an election to a single regiment had better remain out of the army, on the presumption that if he is unpopular with those who have every opportunity of knowing about him, he would most likely be an unpopular officer with the men, and consequently be a detriment to the service. Nominally the German army is the most democratic institution in Europe, for all able-bodied men must serve in it, without distinction of race, color, or rank. As a matter of fact, the veto power which a regimental mess has upon would-be members is not a serious deterrent to candidates, because, as a rule, the man who desires to become an officer usually has friends in some regiment of the service; and it is only fair to say that no German regiment would ever exclude a man without reasons which would be considered valid by the Department of War. The present rules, however, have this advantage, that they create among the officers of a regiment not merely the feeling that they are parts of a great machine, but that they are a social organization bound together by ties as intimate as those uniting a lodge of Freemasons;

that they have to stand one by the other in peace and war, and that the honor of one is the honor of all. The regiments of the German army differ as families differ. In some regiments names reproduce themselves for centuries back, and also groups of names, showing that the traditions of social life have passed down from one generation to another in one unbroken line from a time when Prussia was merely a province of the Roman Empire. Life in a regimental mess is so intimate that the admission to it of an outsider is a matter of grave debate on the part of all members, from the colonel down; and the greatest pains are taken that the candidate shall sustain the traditions which the regiment has accumulated. When the German officer becomes a member of a regiment, almost all his actions are influenced by the opinion of his superior officers — even matrimony. No officer can marry without the consent of his colonel, and this consent can be obtained only after a careful inquiry into all the circumstances surrounding the proposed alliance. First, is the young lady suitable for association with the wives of the other officers? Secondly, will the bridegroom be able to live respectably and bring up his family? Thirdly, are his means or those of his wife invested in proper securities, so that he is not liable to be expelled by reason of bankruptcy? These precautions seem exceed-

THE "SUB"

ingly paternal, but I am assured that they prevent a great deal of unhappiness, for a young officer is very apt to contract matrimony without reference to the future means of support; and, moreover, is apt to be more rash than he would be if he could see himself through the eyes of more experienced men.

This paternal care is also illustrated by the attitude of German military authorities in regard to the duel. Fighting is happily rare amongst German officers, owing to its discouragement by the present emperor, and the regulations governing the appeal to the sword. The German army has decided that all duelling is wrong, and that it can only be condoned in cases where every other remedy has been tried and found insufficient. German officers have courts of honor convened for the special purpose of entertaining charges which would lead to a duel; before these courts only the most delicate personal matters are tried, and the question determined as to how far an apology can be brought about or a duel avoided. Any officer who ventures upon a duel without having received first the consent of a court of honor renders himself liable to immediate disgrace by dismissal. It is safe to say that these courts of honor do an enormous amount towards making duelling difficult, if not impossible.

The social position of the German officers

is the most coveted in Germany. This is not
merely because as a rule German officers spring
from ancient or noble families, or that their regimental messes are very paternally managed, so
as to exclude undesirable elements. He is recognized, over and above that, as of a superior
training intellectually, as a hard worker, and one
to whom the nation looks for defence in case of
war. A foreign invasion is at all times so present to the mind of the German that the army
never for a moment loses its great significance
to the people. With us, our men are so far away
on the outskirts of civilization that we scarcely
hear of them, and many an American has grown
to manhood without being able to describe the
uniform of the American army. The German
officer always wears his uniform, and wherever
he moves represents the majesty of the law as
well as the national power. If a landlord wishes
to recommend his beer-room to you, he can
say nothing higher than that it is frequented by
officers. A theatre in which officers do not appear is considered to have sunk below the level
of good society. Officers at German dinners and
balls are much coveted, for the officer is assumed
to have good-breeding, and to be in all respects
a cultivated man. During the great military
operations in the autumn, officers are quartered
upon the proprietors of the neighborhood, and
far from this being regarded as a nuisance, those

UHLAN OFFICER IN FIELD TRIM

who have officers billeted upon them consider the circumstance rather agreeable than otherwise. When parades and reviews are the order of the day, when traffic is blocked upon the streets, the friendship of an officer is more than sentimental pleasure, for he can take you through all the lines which the police hold against the great army of citizens. An officer can go anywhere in uniform, and enjoys social advantages from the very moment of putting on his shoulder-straps which men in other walks of life do not attain until they have distinguished themselves very much indeed. It is in Germany a great thing to go to court, and very few ever succeed in entering that charmed circle excepting through the army. An officer goes to court as a matter of course, although if his wife is not of a certain rank she may be excluded. In England pretty much everybody goes to court who chooses to incur the expense of the court dress, and all Americans that come to London are presented to the queen if they choose. The late Mr. William Walter Phelps remarked recently that in Germany no American had been presented at court in eighteen years, unless by special request either of the Department of State or for some corresponding official reason. This gives one an idea of the enormous importance attaching in Germany to the mere formal presentation to the sovereign, which causes so much heart-burning amongst those who cannot get it.

The extraordinary social advantages enjoyed by the German officer, and the pecuniary responsibility growing naturally from such advantage, make his small pay, which amounts only to about a dollar a day in the case of a first lieutenant, appear even smaller than it is. An American lady who had been spending a winter in Dresden told me that all the bachelors of the garrison were furnished with a list of marriageable women, each name ornamented with the property she might be expected to inherit. This, I have no doubt, was a mistake on her part, but it is a very common one. German officers stationed in desirable towns are very apt to get into debt, and have to choose between leaving the army in disgrace or marrying a rich girl. This explains why it is that so many officers in Germany have married Jewesses, in spite of the fact that no Jew can become an officer. I do not pretend that German officers are more mercenary than those of other armies, but as there are so many of them, nearly 30,000 in time of peace, the number of bad ones must necessarily be great. The same tendency I have heard complained of in the English army, where the pay is correspondingly small and the social demands equally great. From my own experience in Germany the officers would appear to have married for love, and to be very happy

THE OFFICERS' MESS

in consequence. The number of those who get into debt and fail to secure a rich wife is considerable, although it makes no particular ripple on the surface; such men simply disappear, and turn up sooner or later in America, where they take employment as coachmen, waiters, teachers, or instructors in riding-schools. The change of life is very violent, and is adopted only as preferable to suicide.

The number of German officers one sees on the streets is remarkably small compared to the size of the garrison, and the explanation of this fact is that they are too hard at work to have any time for exhibiting themselves. At four o'clock in the morning, during the favorable seasons of the year, they are up and in the saddle, out with their men drilling them with all their might; their afternoon is occupied with barrack-work, reports, and a lot of odds and ends of routine work, which leaves them pretty well tired out when evening arrives. In France, Russia, Italy, and Austria officers seem to have very much more time on their hands, to judge by the appearance of the streets alone. In England and America the officer may be regarded as having great difficulty in employing his time so as not to be bored, unless he is a singular character, regarded by his comrades as rather a "dig," or one riding a hobby. The German officer not only has an amount of daily routine work far in excess of what is customary in other armies, but he has to prepare for periodical examinations upon which his promotion depends. This, perhaps, explains why in society the German officer is found to know usually one or more languages besides his own. Last month I met at dinner a German officer of the artillery who was not even on the Great General Staff, and discovered by accident that he understood and used six foreign languages, namely, Russian, Polish, English, French, Scandinavian, and Italian. He was a man of means, yet constantly working at some new subject for the mere love of improvement.

The swagger of the officer on the street, which strikes the travelling Anglo-Saxon, can be compared to that of the university student, who puts upon his head a little cap about the size of a saucer, and parades the street in a costume intended to arrest the attention of others by its ridiculousness. The very young officer is apt to swagger because of the novelty he enjoys in wearing a uniform for the first time, but this swagger is rarely maintained excepting amongst cavalry officers, who are mostly recruited from the wealthier aristocracy, and are not presumed to bring with them as much intellectual weight as the rest of the army. The German school-boy is kept in a species of slavery from the time he is seven years of age to the moment when he either goes to the university or becomes an officer. During these

FIELD DRILL OF PRUSSIAN INFANTRY

years of hard mental training he is almost entirely deprived of any opportunity to develop himself either in the field of sports or in society. The transition, therefore, is most violent when, from the nursery as it were, he is suddenly placed upon the highest level of social consideration by investing himself with epaulets. That he should not make a fool of himself on many occasions is unreasonable to expect, and it is only a source of wonder that he so soon conquers the natural tendency of an inexperienced man.

In the autumn of every year, when the bulk of the crops has been harvested, so that troops may march across country without doing very much damage to crops, the whole of the German army, including a large proportion of reserves who are called in for special training, may be said to appear in the field on a war footing. Instead of sending a regiment or so to spend a few weeks sheltered by canvas, the whole country becomes alive with marching companies and regiments, marching sometimes hundreds of miles to meet an imaginary enemy, as though war had been declared. During these marches they skirmish with detachments sent to meet them; they have to guard against attack by night as well as by day; they have to provide for forage and food as though in actual war; they quarter themselves as best they can in villages, and often sleep out in the open with no protection over their heads, and none beneath them unless they can find some straw to lie upon. The annual mobilization of troops all over the country, amounting to about half a million of men, is a serious source of expense, which is, however, cheerfully borne, because it is recognized to be the only means of teaching a soldier his duty in the presence of an enemy. So far as I know, the only work done in our army that corresponds in any degree to that in the German is that represented by the long marches which General Miles initiated in our Southwestern country amongst our cavalry, sending them hundreds of miles through the wilderness, liable not only to capture by the rival columns of United States troops, but also to actual destruction by Apaches. Any one who has seen the thoroughly business-like way in which our cavalry does its duty as compared with the methods of such of our troops as are quartered in or about large towns, without any corresponding training, will quickly appreciate the distinction between the real soldier and the make-believe one. Each year in Germany, over and above the infinite number of small field operations, there is one on a larger scale, commonly referred to as the grand manœuvres, which takes place when all the scattered garrisons representing one army corps unite in order of battle against another army corps gathered together in the same way. From the time of a

AN OFFICER OF ARTILLERY

company's leaving its garrison to the time when it becomes part of an army corps the distance marched may be two or three hundred miles, and the time occupied two or three months, according to circumstances. These grand manœuvres are always attended by the emperor in person, who commands now on one side and now on the other, testing the efficiency of every branch of his service as thoroughly as is possible without the use of ball-cartridge. When one bears in mind that a single army corps marching along a single road occupies for its 30,000 men between thirty and forty miles, it is easy to see how much complication can be produced by attempting to bring those men rapidly to the front in line of battle, extending, perhaps, ten miles between the extremities of the two wings. Then, too, there are the difficulties in the way of bringing up to each company or battalion the ammunition and food supplies, quartering the men, providing them with water, and keeping them fit for the next day's hard work. These problems never enter into the manœuvres undertaken at Peekskill or Aldershot, where the men return to the same quarters every night. The German officer knows that aside from his professional knowledge as tested by paper examinations, his promotion and general career as an officer will be largely modified by the work which he does during the autumn manœuvres.

He may know his theoretical strategy by heart, but if he plants his battery too far one way or the other, if he neglects to seize the right position, if he leads his cavalry into a swamp, if he brings his men under a fire where they may presumably expect annihilation, if he does a hundred things which in real war would be fatal, and against which no text-books can protect him, he is immediately the object of severe criticism by the commander-in-chief. The field is studded with experienced officers who act solely as umpires, riding from one detachment to the other, and making minute notes of everything which they see. The great war game is played under certain rules which military experience has shown to be well devised, based upon experience in actual war, and when these rules are violated the officer may expect to suffer in consequence. The troops taking part in these manœuvres have no previous knowledge of the country over which they are to operate, and therefore their officers have to become as practised in the use of map and compass as a sailor at sea. They are told simply that between two points several hundreds of miles apart a battle may be reasonably expected — much as though a column of our troops were ordered to march from New York to Pittsburg on a certain day, having only the information that within a hundred miles of the latter place resistance might

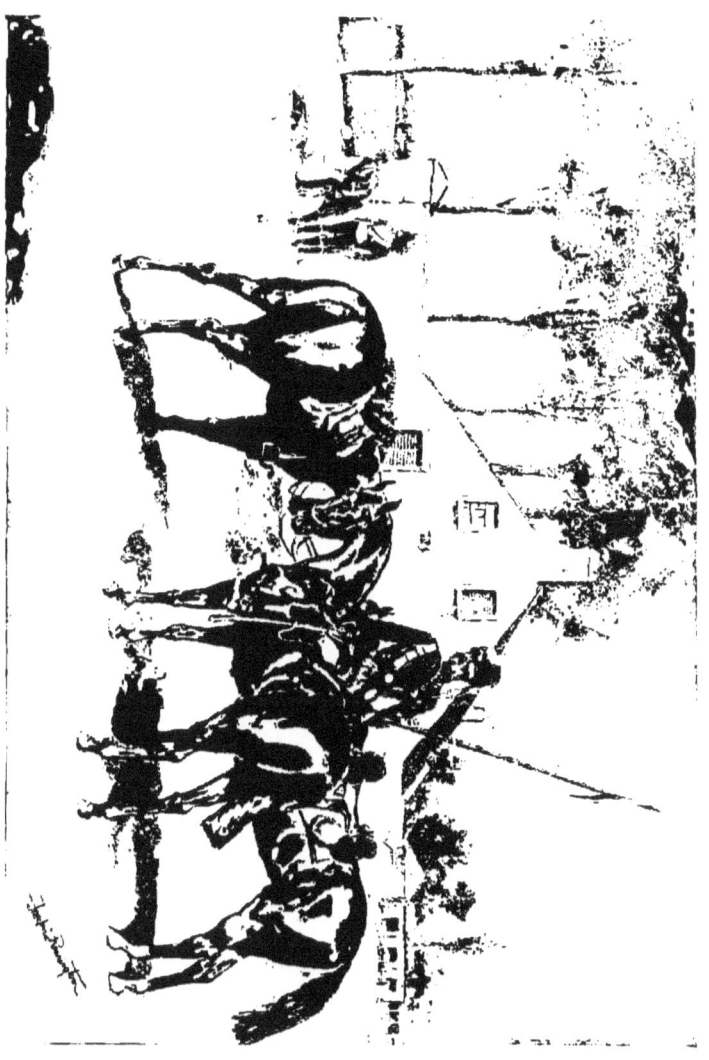

HUSSARS SCOUTING

be expected from a certain force. Of course in Germany the very best maps are at the service of the officers—maps on the scale of about one mile to the inch. These maps are made by the government, and sold at a very small price. During the grand manœuvres it is the custom of the commander-in-chief, after the day's work is concluded, to sound the bugle-call that assembles all the officers about him—at least as many as can come; he then delivers what is called the critique, a general critical summary of the day's work. The present emperor is particularly noted for the thoroughness with which he conducts his critiques; his memory is extraordinary, his knowledge of soldiers' detail work equally so, and he has besides the physical energy that enables him to overlook nearly every part of the great battlefield. This is an advantage which makes his critical discussions much more dreaded even than those of his grandfather, who in his latter years was naturally unable to attend manœuvres more than in a somewhat perfunctory manner.

For the officers and men in general the manœuvres afford little amusement. They have to be up long before the sun, their work all day is of the hardest kind, they are quartered in stables and peasants' houses almost as comfortless as the bare ground, and if they have any hours of leisure they are not where they could possibly enjoy any social relaxation, but in fact the care of their men must necessarily occupy all their time, to say nothing of preparations for the morrow.

It is a little better for those who are immediately in the suite of the emperor, either as guests or as officers commanded to headquarters, as, for instance, the inspectors of different departments, the umpires, and high officers of other army corps. These have no great responsibilities after the day's fighting closes, and at once return to the headquarters in some town, where they are properly lodged and fed. The emperor usually gives a dinner every evening to the principal

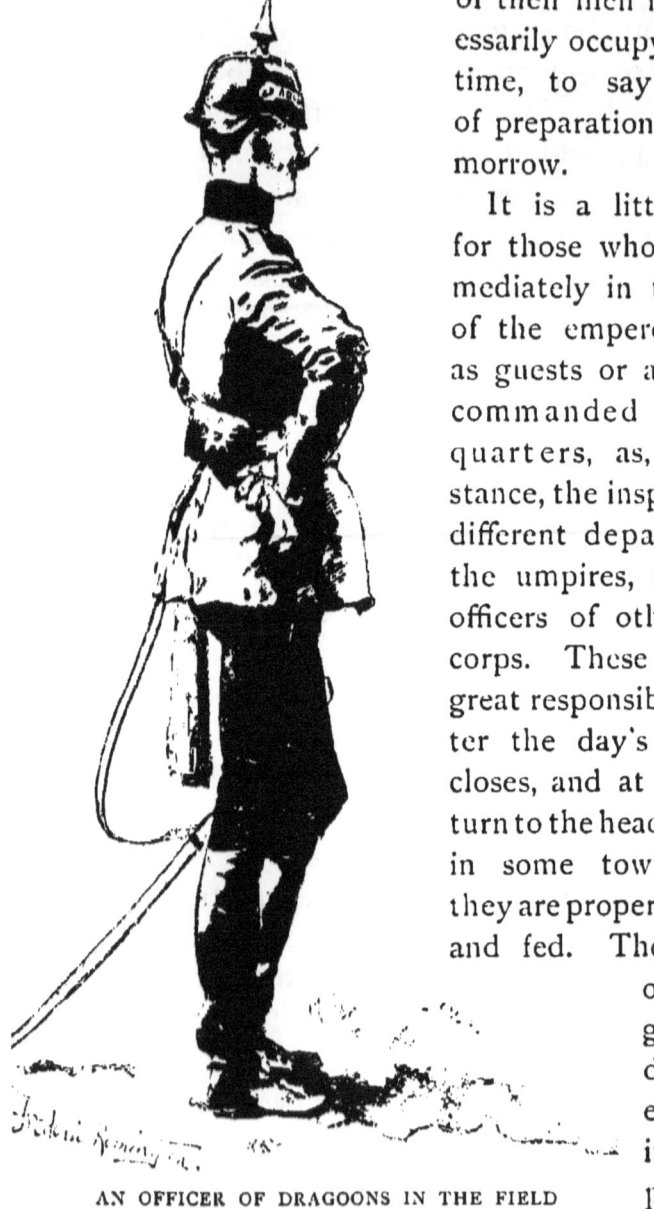

AN OFFICER OF DRAGOONS IN THE FIELD

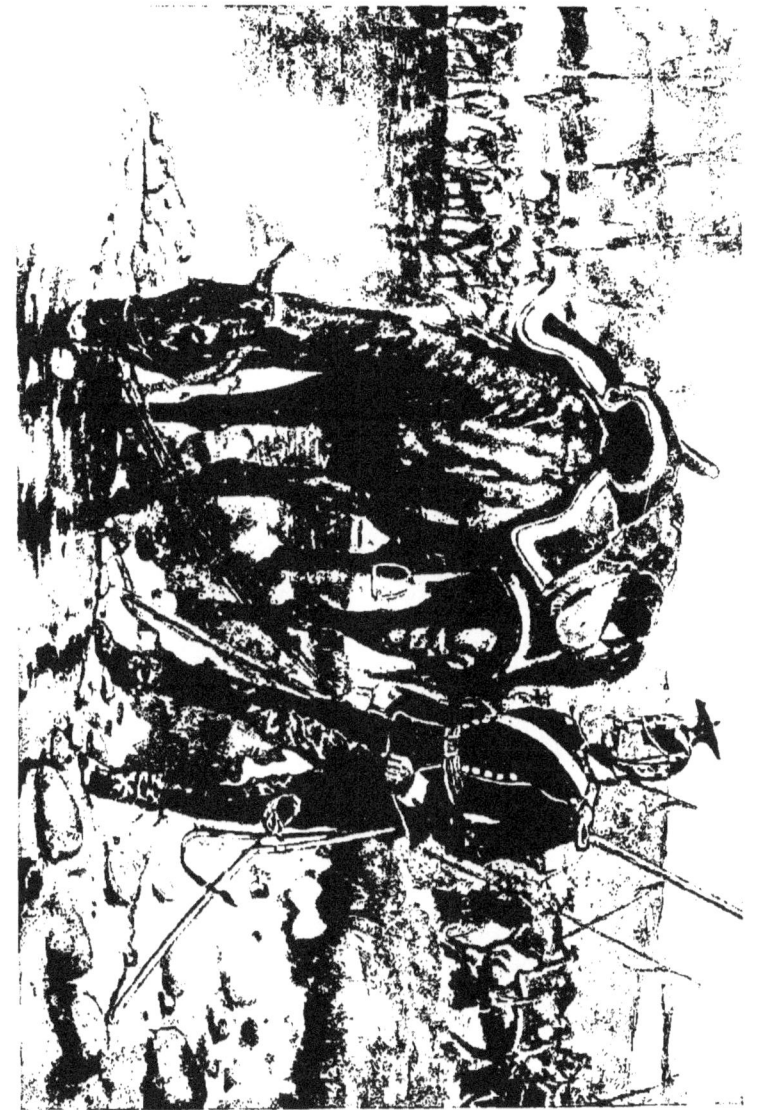
CAVALRYMAN WATERING HIS HORSE

officers and officials in the neighborhood, as well as to the principal citizens residing near by. He seizes the opportunity of the grand manœuvres to make the acquaintance personally of the principal people in the different sections of his country, and combines politics with war in an efficient way. The social features of the grand manœuvres do very much to bring notable people of different parts of the country together, and thus little by little to efface the jealousies which naturally exist among citizens of the different states who have only been united since the Franco-German war. The year 1892 was the first in the reign of the present emperor that had no imperial or grand manœuvres, for the obvious reason that cholera was present in many German towns, and particularly in France close to the German border. They will probably, however, take place this year—1893—as usual, and in the neighborhood of where they should have been last year, namely, about Metz. It is much to be hoped that they will be carried out so as to bring the people of this province into contact with the emperor and his surroundings. The result cannot fail to at least modify those feelings of antipathy which people of the lately French provinces are still said to entertain for their German conqueror. The French press persists in nurturing the idea that Germans are more or less coarse and cruel masters, and that Alsace and Lorraine cannot long remain separated from the land of Napoleon. Nothing will do more to alter any such feeling than to come into personal relations with the chief of the German nation, and to see the manner in which he handles troops. He commands with a skill that does not encourage the idea of Alsace and Lorraine changing hands during his lifetime at least.

The German officer does remarkably little in the way of athletics or sport of any kind; the main reasons are that he is short both of time and of money, particularly of time. The training to the eye and the judgment which comes from cross-country riding over hedges and ditches in pursuit of a fox or a deer would be a very valuable addition to the accomplishments of the German officer of to-day. Among the crack cavalry regiments there is considerable steeplechasing, but, on account of the expense, it is limited to those who have large means. It is a rare thing for an officer to take part in rowing, sailing, bicycling, football, cricket, tennis, baseball, golf, or any of the games which do so much to render a man master of his muscles. The present emperor has done very much to make sport popular and fashionable. He realizes fully the advantages which a man brought up to athletic games has over one who has only the training of the professional soldier, but I fear it will

A JOLLY PARTY BY THE WAY-SIDE

take a generation educated differently from the present to bring about a reform so much to be desired. The evil commences during the school years.

The German boy, up to his eighteenth or nineteenth year, when he leaves school, is looked upon merely as a machine for grinding out Latin, Greek, and mathematics. If he has in each week two or three hours devoted to gymnastic exercises, he considers himself fortunate. It never enters his head that he should spend at least three hours a day in out-door games of some kind. His teachers hold up their hands in horror at the idea of devoting as much attention to the physical culture of their pupils as to the cramming of their minds with dead knowledge. Even my excellent German tutor who fitted me for Yale, and who was himself a teacher of gymnastics, regarded it as monstrous that boys should spend two or three hours a day in playing football or rowing. The whole professorial caste of Germany, loyal as it is to the Hohenzollerns, regards this emperor with ill-disguised suspicion because of his desire that the German school-boy should be a typically vigorous creature as well as an educated one. The drudgery of the school-boy's life can scarcely be credited by one who has not lived it, and it is only because the emperor has suffered under it that he is now so strong an advocate for improvement.

The injury to health, which is the direct result of the unnatural life led by the German boy, has become strangely apparent in late years,. through published statistics; but even without them the evils manifest themselves to impartial eyes in the difficulty of getting men of proper build to fill the ranks of the officers' corps. If the War Department accomplishes nothing more than to bring pressure upon the academic bodies in this one direction, it will have justified its existence; and if the present emperor should die having done nothing greater than to leave every school-child the right to physical development as well as mental, he will have earned the gratitude of every mother and school-child in the fatherland. Already football clubs, rowing clubs, sailing clubs, are in existence, and are destined to increase in number and importance. Germany has made enormous strides in the last ten years in the field of sport, and shows no signs of going backwards. German oarsmen and bicyclists are making excellent records; they take to sport naturally wherever they are afforded the opportunities, and as soon as the school-boy is allowed his afternoons free for out-door exercise, there is no reason to doubt that the German fields will be studded with active lads hard at their games, exactly as in every Anglo-Saxon community to-day; nor is there any reason to suppose that in consequence of this liberty the German will prove less able to defend his country, or hold his own as a manufacturer or merchant or professional man in competition with those of other countries.

When the schoolboy becomes the student or the officer, he immediately practises fencing very assiduously to defend what he is pleased to call his honor, and he is very apt to conclude that only an officer or a student is possessed of such an ornament. This exercise of swordsmanship is very good as far as it goes; but, judging by the appearance of the students who indulge most in this manly exercise, beer-drinking forms so large a

A DRAGOON TRUMPETER

share of the work done as to almost neutralize the benefits claimed for it. The fencing takes place mostly in rooms dense with tobacco smoke, dust, and human exhalation, and does not compare for physical benefit to a game of baseball or football. It would assist very much in dissipating a great deal of nonsense in Germany if students at the universities could measure their prowess by competing for prizes in outdoor sports where previous training of a severe kind has to be undergone.

The influence of the German officer upon German life and sport is so great that we can hardly imagine sport to become thoroughly popular in the fatherland until clubs are formed among the officers, and thus made fashionable. The beginning to this better state of things has been made by the emperor, who is not only a good yachtsman, oarsman, huntsman, tennis-player, but even threatens to sail a canoe. When his views in regard to the physical education of men and boys become general among his subjects, we may look for a development of the German officer that shall bring him to a considerably higher level than even at present.

In theory the German soldier has substantially the same legal guarantees in regard to his rights and personal liberty as the private of the United States regular army or of England. Any officer is liable to court-martial if he addresses his supe-

CUIRASSIER ON STAFF DUTY

rior officer in language that is unprofessional, exactly as it is with us. Practically, however, the German officer often reprimands his stupid subordinate by a cuff on the ears, which the victim receives with equanimity. In fact, he would rather have the cuff and have done with it in a few minutes, than be tried in a more legal form and punished by arrest for days, perhaps weeks. Germans are irritable, as all people of great brain activity are, and in a moment of excitement use language that is unparliamentary and administer a box on the ears with striking rapidity. The laws governing the army are very strict in enforcing the proper treatment of the soldier by his superior, particular stress being laid on the necessity of maintaining the self-respect of the soldier.

Whoever takes the trouble to attend the manœuvres of French or Russian army corps must be surprised by the many precautions taken to prevent their seeing anything. In Germany, on the contrary, I am able to say, from having attended all the grand manœuvres during the present reign, that no one bothers his head about who may or may not be among the spectators. There are, of course, a number of field gendarmes, who are detailed to protect the spectators from sudden charges of cavalry, and to keep order; but it never enters their head that they are to arrest a Frenchman or a Russian, whether he

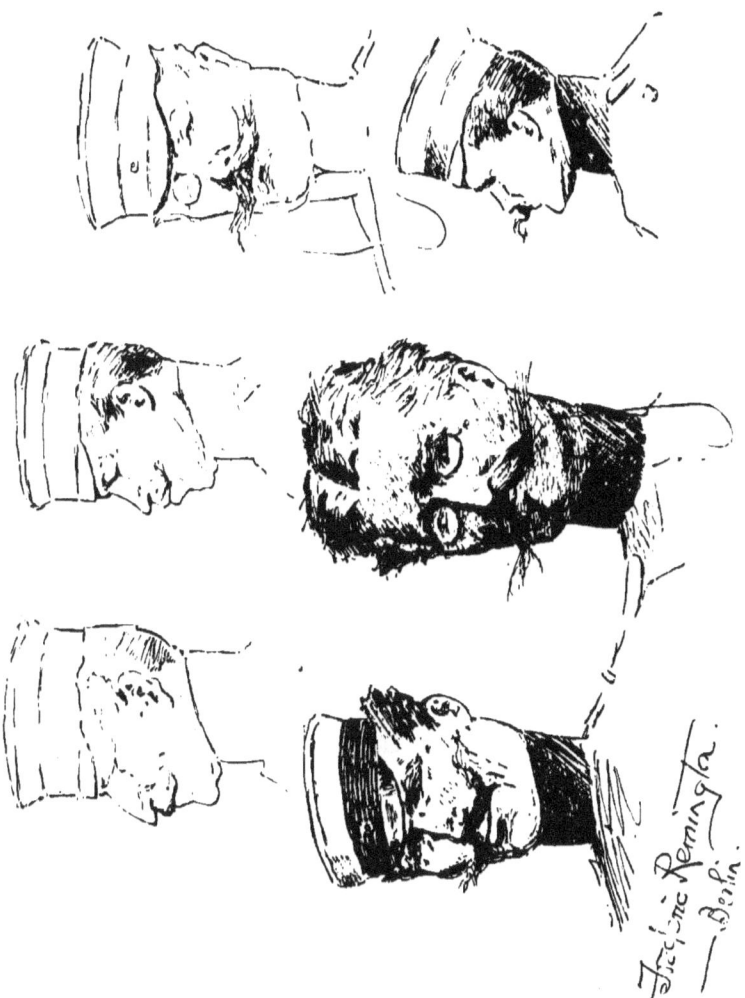

be a spy or not. Whenever the German troops operate near the frontier, it is well known that many of the French officers swell the crowd of spectators; every one knows that they are French officers dressed up as civilians; in fact, the story is told of a humorous gendarme who was clearing the road, and addressed the crowd in front of him as follows: "Gentlemen and Messieurs the French officers will please move on." The explanation of this apparent indifference on the part of German war authorities in regard to being scrutinized by their enemies lies in the fact that they know pretty well everything that their enemies know in regard to their neighbors, and they are equally confident that their enemies are pretty well informed about German affairs. If it should come to a war, they are willing to depend upon the superiority of their organization, and, above all, on the superiority of the material composing their army, both officers and men, particularly the officers.

MOUNTED HUSSAR

# EMPEROR WILLIAM'S STUD-FARM AND HUNTING FOREST

WHEN Remington and I crossed into Germany we determined to make an excursion into the very easternmost corner of the Prussian monarchy, where the father of Frederick the Great established a great horse-breeding establishment near a little village called Trakehnen. This famous studfarm is still carried on with characteristic en-

ergy, and not only provides the German army with the hundred thousand horses which it requires in time of peace, but does an enormous amount towards keeping up in the country a high standard of horse for general purposes. Trakehnen is only about ten miles from the Russian frontier, and has three times been exposed to capture by invasion from over the border; but each time the authorities have been able to escape with all the animals there, a feat which appears almost miraculous considering the flat and open character of the country. I had with me a letter of introduction to the commandant or governor of this estate, Major von Frankenberg-Proschlitz. We alighted one beautiful day in July at the little station of Trakehnen. It was the only house in sight, the village was four miles away, but the major had kindly sent an open carriage to meet us. The drive to the major's house was along beautiful avenues shaded by oak-trees almost the whole way. When we halted at the front door, our host received us with every manifestation of good-will, in spite of the fact that on the morrow he was anticipating an official inspection at the hands of no less impressive dignitaries than the minister of war and his colleague of the Agricultural Department. A Prussian inspection is a matter of tremendous importance, and that Major von Frankenberg under such circumstances should appear comfortable, even genial, speaks volumes for the self-reliance and sweetness of that gentleman's nature.

Nothing more pretty can be conceived than the appearance of the major's quarters as we drove up through the vista of trees. It was large, commodious, covered with vines, fragrant

COLTS PLAYING NEAR A HERD

with the odor of flowers that grew about and before the door. A shady lawn stretched in the rear with flower beds on its edges, and close by was a delightful arbor where coffee was served in the afternoon during the warm season. Within a few minutes the family of this Prussian officer made us feel that we had once more fallen amongst good friends. The kind major quickly divined the interest which we felt in the great horse-breeding establishment which he controlled, and as soon as luncheon was disposed of lost no time in driving us about from point to point, chatting with us in regard to what we saw, and answering our questions with frankness.

To begin with, Trakehnen is situated in the most favored province of Germany for horse-breeding purposes, although, geographically considered, it appears to be the most unpropitious. Nearly every farm in East Prussia is devoted to this one occupation, and the German army gets many more horses from this little corner than any other province or kingdom of the empire. The war authorities are, in respect to this branch of the government, very liberal, for it affects the army directly as well as it does the country indirectly. The very best thoroughbreds that can be bought for money are brought here, and from them are bred a secondary class of horses which the Germans call "halbblut," a word which cannot be safely translated as half-breed, but is more nearly rendered by the French "près du sang." Every year some of the best names on the English turf disappear in favor of the breeding-farms for the German cavalry. The stallions chosen are such as have good records on the race-track, and, in addition, the peculiar qualities of form and structure which the German officer considers essential to the ideal cavalry horse—that is to say, one in whom speed and weight-carrying capacity unite to the highest possible degree. All told, Trakehnen has about a thousand head of every age, but of only one general class. It has been by strict adherence to the principle of selection above mentioned that the *Trakehner* or *Prussian* horse has reached its present definite position and high level of power. Remington's drawings will give a better notion of the ideal which the Prussian military authorities entertain on the subject of this horse than any lengthy description which I might attempt. Suffice it to say that Germans at least consider themselves amply compensated for the cost of this institution during the two centuries of its existence.

The major does not breed for the race-track nor for the plough; he has in view the heavy cavalry cuirassier horse, or the requirements of the lighter hussar, and Trakehnen may be considered a national stud-farm, in so far as the horse required for the cavalry is one that is useful for other purposes as well.

MASSAGE OF A COLT'S KNEES

We pulled up in a field in which were a hundred three-year-old stallions running free and watched by two herders, each bearing a long whip, which he cracked now and then as a warning that some one of the herd was straying. The herders had no saddles or stirrups, sat simply upon a blanket strapped to the horse's back, and were dressed in the livery of the estate, which is not dissimilar to the grooms' livery of the royal family. Any one familiar with three-year-old stallions in English or American stables might easily expect that a herd of one hundred would be disposed to resent the intrusion of a couple of strangers in their midst, especially remembering that these colts were of thorough-bred parents, at least on one side, and of fair blood on the other. We naturally remarked that the herd appeared very quiet, and paid little attention to our carriage as it drove up close to them on the grass. The major wished us, however, to understand that they were as gentle as sheep and not half as shy, and, in order to make a practical test of this, I jumped from my seat and walked up to the herd, into the very midst of them, strolling in and out amongst them, patting them on the nose or on the flank, wherever I happened to be nearest them. Amongst German cavalry horses I had often experienced an extraordinary amount of docility, which comes naturally as the result of intelligent handling on the part of the grooms, and was therefore more or less prepared to risk the heels and the teeth of those into whose midst Major von Frankenberg requested me to wander.

If this docility sprang from sleepiness or coarseness of blood, there would be little worth noting, but in the case of animals of most unquestioned pluck and power the experience is certainly unique.

"How do you accomplish this result?" we asked.

A "TRAKEHNER" HORSE-WRANGLER

"We offer a prize," answered the major, "to those whose horses show the most confiding disposition at the approach of man. Whenever I enter the large spaces under roof where they are gathered for the night, if I discover the least shyness or unfriendliness on the part of the colts, it is a sign that the herdsmen have acted contrary to their duty."

Every spring, usually about May, the four-year-olds are distributed amongst the auxiliary or secondary stud-farms of Prussia, likewise for breeding purposes, so that with the exception of the stallions and brood-mares all the good blood here is disposed of when it is four years old. There is a very formidable committee that determines what horses are to be reserved for military breeding purposes at the other stations and what shall be sold at auction, an event which draws to Trakehnen buyers from every country of the globe, anxious to secure specimens of this excellent breed of horse. It is from this estate that the emperor draws the horses which he uses for private purposes in his carriages and for the saddle.

By a special arrangement, made in 1848, the Prussian crown made these estates a present to the government, on condition that each year the king should be allowed to select thirty horses for private use, and naturally those selected are apt to be the best. A beautiful little saddle-horse was being trained for the emperor's eldest son during our visit, as well-built an animal as one could wish, and as gentle as a baby. The royal stables of Prussia are filled almost exclusively with black horses for driving purposes, although for riding the emperor does not confine himself to any particular color. In addition to the breeding animals which are sent from here to the various stud-farms of the government in other parts of Prussia, the government is very wise and generous in encouraging horse-breeding in the neighborhood by every possible means. The farmers are permitted the use of government stallions of excellent pedigree at a remarkably low figure—$5 was, I believe, the current price last year.

The secret of Trakehnen's fame as a horse-breeding place, according to our host, is the fact that it is irrigated in every direction in such a manner that the grass is rich and sweet to an extraordinary extent. The soil, too, is most favorable—deep and spongy. When it was originally selected for this purpose it was nothing better than a vast swamp over which the moose roamed wild, as he still roams in a circumscribed section of the Baltic shores near the mouth of the Memel River. The father of Frederick the Great was a capital farmer, and had a good eye for horses as well. He converted this swamp into the richest pasture-land of Germany, where even to-day one cannot dig two feet without

BRINGING OUT A STALLION

striking water. In winter the meadows are flooded, and only the most careful irrigation preserves them in good condition for the balance of the year. There are no fences anywhere upon the estate, which stretches about nine miles in one direction and three or four in the other, and were the horses less docile than they are, it would seem an easy thing for them to get lost many times in the year.

Major von Frankenberg has an enormous admiration for this particular horse, and as he goes to England every year for the purpose of selecting thorough-breds, and has visited the stud-farms of nearly every country in the world, it is fair to conclude that his feelings are not the result of bias.

"But," said he, "I insist on one indispensable condition—our horse must not be used until he is six years old. He must be allowed to get his growth and seasoning before using. We made a great mistake in 1870 in permitting many young horses, as young as four years of age, to come into the army. They nearly all broke down, and in the long-run were a source of great loss to us—far beyond their cost. With proper food and treatment, however, I will back him against any horse I know."

The major gave us many illustrations of what the *Trakehner* has done in his experience; not such rides as Austrian and German officers performed in October of 1892, but work of practical value. For instance, in the campaign against France of 1870 and 1871, he led his regiment of hussars throughout the months of January, February, and March, over a country covered with ice and snow, at the rate of thirty-five English miles a day.

At the same time the major was careful to point out what United States cavalry officers can appreciate more than those of any other army, that these are not horses that can be turned out to take care of themselves, like the Indian's mustang or the rough Cossack pony of the steppes.

All the young horses are carefully rubbed clean and inspected every day, the brush and currycomb being used in cleaning. During this process the young colts are tied, but when three or four years old they stand quietly enough and enjoy it. In order to insure docility on the part of these animals it is made a rule that each day the colts are to be stroked with the hand, their feet raised — in other words, treated in such a way as to make them familiar with their future masters.

It would seem as though the rich, succulent grass produced by the pastures would be enough food for these young animals, but the major said that they did better when they received two portions of oats a day, once in the morning and again at noon, but never at night.

THE RIDE THROUGH THE WOOD WITH THE OLD FORESTER

One evening the major took us to see the horses called home from the pasture. They came in troops of hundreds, and gathered in large enclosures facing the stables, or rather the large spaces in which they all spent the night in common, in groups of one hundred or less. These paddocks were formed by planting railway sleepers on end at short intervals, connected by gas-pipes — a very simple and economical arrangement. Here the young horses are exercised in the winter when it would·be unsuitable to let them out in the snow. They go round and round in a ring under the eye of the groom.

On the occasion of our visit I noticed that the main body divided itself according to color—the blacks going to one corner, the browns to another, the bays to a third; of whites or grays I saw no specimens. Here and there would be one who had mistaken his corner, or was seeking forbidden company out of deviltry. The keeper had no difficulty in bringing him to his right senses, however, by simply calling his name and waving his hand in the direction of the corner to which he belonged. The colt thus addressed invariably leaped out from the corner in which he was an intruder, and galloped straight to the corner whose color matched his. This we saw done many times over, and it never failed. . . .

Neither Remington nor I had intended to tax the hospitality of our kindly host more than a day, but we were gladly persuaded to prolong our stay, which gave us an opportunity to visit the vast and almost primeval forests to which the Emperor of Germany retires in order to hunt the wild deer and boar. A victoria was placed at our disposal by the major, and in this luxurious vehicle we sat while a pair of black Trakehner mares carried us swiftly, and without interruption, over the twenty miles of country road that separated us from the hunting-lodge of Rominten. It was a rolling open country across which we drove, until we came upon the edges of sombre woods. The cultivation was on all sides of a high grade, and in striking contrast to what prevails across the border, only about five or ten miles distant. There were few villages, but their inhabitants were clean and tidily dressed. Had it not been a day of sunshine, made more beautiful by the effect of fleecy clouds studding here and there the blue heavens, in an atmosphere freshened by the breeze following a day of rain, with a road under us neither dusty nor muddy, although towards the latter part of it it was a mere cart-track through a somewhat sandy soil, I fear that we might have termed our twenty miles rather desolate travelling. We saw some fine specimens of the emperor's wild-boar and big red deer, that bounded into the thicket as we approached, for these animals are not as tame as those in English parks,

ARREST OF A POACHER IN THE FOREST

being rarely disturbed. At one point our driver stopped to let us get out and see how near we could come to a herd that appeared to be about a thousand yards off. We stalked so close that Remington decided emphatically that he would have bagged half a dozen had he been allowed to try his hand at it. As it was, however, he did something better by making some sketches from behind a fallen tree. We drove a long distance, after this, amidst magnificent trees, mostly evergreens, although oak and poplar appeared here and there. The forest, which includes about fifty square miles, is watered by some excellent streams, stocked with a variety of fish, chief of all the trout, although pike, perch, carp, *Scardinious erythrophthalmus*, *Carassius vulgaris*, and many others of excellent quality are also abundant. Half a dozen houses compose all there is of the village here, whose inhabitants are principally occupied in work about the forest. We passed through the village, over a bridge, and up a hill, on the top of which stood the house which the emperor is building as his hunting-lodge. The dark evergreen forest closes it in at the rear, and in many respects it suggests a summer residence in the Adirondack Mountains. There were several officials in the house at the time, on various errands, the most important to us being the forester. We asked permission to enter and take a look at the rooms, but were politely informed, with apparent regret, that this was contrary to their orders. The German court was, however, at Potsdam, and, as there was a telegraph office near by, we wired to the capital asking permission of the emperor to visit his place here. The postmaster and chief of the telegraph department we found perched on the ridge-pole of his thatched roof making some repairs. He came down cheerfully from the roof, sent off our message for us, and acceded to our desire that he should harness up his ponies to a farm wagon and point out to us some interesting features of the wilderness. We had a rather bumpy ride of it, for our way led over rocks and stumps, zigzagging in and out among the big trees without reference to any road or path. He was a pretty old man, this forester, bent by rheumatism as well as years, but withal of a communicative and kindly disposition. As the emperor's house here is so near the Russian frontier, it naturally occurred to Remington that a party of enterprising Muscovite cowboys could, without difficulty, on some moonlight night, jump this ranch, so to speak, and carry off the emperor a hostage to St. Petersburg, without any more difficulty than cutting the telegraph wires leading from Rominten to the main line, some twenty or thirty miles away.

The old forester took us to points where we had glimpses of little lakes and streams and

PEASANTS NEAR ROMINTEN

patches of meadow, surrounded by wilderness as perfect as anything in Colorado, and amused us until it was time to think of our noonday dinner with a running commentary upon his life at Rominten.

His greatest hardship used to be protecting the forest from poachers. He told us that the last head game-keeper here had been shot by a poacher, but remarked, by way of a consoling foot-note, that his successor managed to kill two poachers at one shot. It would seem as though next to impossible to prevent poaching in such a vast forest as this, yet he assured me that with proper organization they had succeeded in almost suppressing this nuisance. The staff of foresters numbers from forty to fifty men, whose principal occupation is the patrolling of the woods, according to preconcerted arrangement, studying trees and plants, and noting everything that affects the welfare of the beasts which provide sport for the emperor and his guests.

It is only since 1890 that the emperor has taken a fancy to this hunting-ground, and, until he built the hunting-lodge for whose inspection we had sought permission, he lived at the little inn where we had ordered dinner, and slept in the very room from the window of which Remington made a sketch of the building. The place appeals strongly to the emperor, because it is so thoroughly natural and wild, in refreshing contrast to many royal parks, where the grass appears to be trimmed by a lawn-mower, and every tree has, so to speak, its hair brushed every morning. William II., too, is the first monarch of Europe who has appreciated the value of American methods of travel, and has so organized his train of cars that he can move from one end of his empire to the other not only without personal fatigue, but under conditions that enable him to transact state business as satisfactorily as if he were in his working-room at Potsdam or Berlin. The Chicago Vestibule Limited finds its counterpart in the German imperial train, which may be said to have doubled the capacity for work of a monarch mainly criticised because of his superabundant energy. People who find

GERMAN PEASANT, EAST PRUSSIA

fault with the emperor because, as they say, he is perpetually rushing from one corner of Europe to the other, forget that it is not he who does the rushing, but the train of cars under him. His life, meanwhile, is as placid and methodical as one could wish, but where his grandfather was satisfied to know a man through a written report, William II. prefers to see that man face to face.

But this is digression. The old forester illustrated the formerly neglected condition of this forest by telling us that thirty years ago there were not more than fifteen head of deer in the whole chase, thanks to neglect and poaching; to-day it is estimated that there are at least one thousand, thanks for which are mainly due to the excellent administration of the late forester who was shot by the poacher. Two months before we visited the place wild-boar had been introduced, and already four young ones had been born on the estate. This will prove an additional attraction for the future, as the wild-boar is notoriously one of the gamiest of animals. There are some moose here as well, differing scarcely at all from those of New Brunswick and Maine, but it is doubtful whether this animal will survive. The sport most relished here is the chase after the big red deer, of which about one hundred and fifty are shot annually. At different points in the forest we came upon racks at which the deer feed during severe winters, when food has to

Some notes from Pite Zominten
Frederic Remington

be provided for them, but they offered nothing in their structure to call for particular comment. Here, as in our first approach to the house, we were struck by the diversity and fine growth of the oak, beech, ash, elm, chestnut, linden, and evergreen trees about us. Also by the great diversity in the surface of the ground, in marked contrast to the rest of the great Prussian plain. There were steep little hills, beautiful gorges, and, travelling as we did, it appeared as though we were in a hilly country, with streams in every valley, the slopes of which had been laid out with consummate art to simulate the Adirondacks.

Wolves, according to our worthy forester, are a great nuisance, and do a vast amount of mischief. Last year the keepers shot a most savage beast, who did an extraordinary amount of injury to the other animals. It seemed impossible to find him until the following plan was adopted: A wide circle was made about the spot in which they knew he must have his hiding-place; this line was marked off by twigs planted in the ground at short intervals. Packthread was then drawn from twig to twig, connecting the whole circle excepting at one point, where an opening was left, near which the hunters stationed themselves. At intervals of ten feet red and yellow bits of rag were hung upon this line, for it was discovered that a wolf will not cross an impediment of this nature, which reminds one of the superstitious feeling the chicken is said to have in regard to crossing a chalk-line. The wolf made his appearance in due course of time, and went from rag to rag in the hope of finding a way out. When he did so, however, it was to fall into the hands of his avengers, who shot him on the 15th day of November, 1891. He was stuffed, and is now scowling, through glass eyes only, in one of the corners of the hunting-lodge —a fine-looking beast, whose acquaintance, however, I should not like to have made under any other circumstances.

Our dinner was quite a festive affair, for in the midst of this wilderness had congregated at one and the same time not only the forester and the major-domo of the palace, but a high economic functionary from Berlin, who was here to make an inspection of the emperor's property. All three received us in the spirit of fellowship, caused perhaps by the fact that on returning to the inn we found a dispatch from the Lord Chamberlain at Potsdam, informing us that the emperor had given us the permission we desired. It was a permission which we had had little reason to anticipate, because an inventory of the place was being made, the furniture was in a somewhat confused state, and clerks were at work on the premises.

This hunting-lodge of the emperor's is a cross between the typical Swiss chalet and an American log house; there is a striking amount of quaint Norwegian carving about it, and the rafters of the roof come to a point in the shape of grinning dragons' heads—a feature of Scandinavian architecture I had noticed at many points in Norway. The emperor took a great fancy to

THE EMPEROR'S HUNTING-LODGE

the simplicity and strength characterizing Norwegian buildings on his many journeys along that coast, and had a dozen Norwegian builders come down on purpose from Christiania in order to erect this house for him. It is, of course, unpainted, and finished in the most severe style, as befits the purpose for which it was originally designed. Inside, the walls and ceilings are all of the natural logs, finished off roughly and stained. The ceilings are low, the rooms small, but every corner is pervaded with coziness. The large assembly or living room looks down a series of rustic terraces to the little valley, where the trout stream runs from the Russian frontier to the Baltic. At one end of this large room is a great double fireplace, about which a large family can gather in the evening for the purpose of spinning hunting-yarns or telling ghost-stories. It is an exact counterpart of the fireplace in many a Norwegian house I have seen, reproduced here with minute fidelity. From the ceiling hangs an elaborate chandelier consisting entirely of antlers, so arranged as to form innumerable holders for candles.

The emperor strongly dislikes anything in the nature of guards when he is on his hunting expeditions, although half a dozen country policemen do duty here when the emperor is present. On his first arrival they were drawn up in line to salute him, but he ordered that it should not happen again, and now they are carefully kept out of sight. He is a man so indifferent to danger or personal safety that the mere idea of having officials watching on his account is in the highest degree distasteful. The furniture of the rooms at Rominten was in harmony with the simplicity of the walls—hard-wood, strongly made, and merely stained, so as to disclose the natural grain, which is, after all, the greatest charm about any furniture. On the walls hung many pictures of hunting scenes, notably the magnificent studies of Landseer. Amongst the pictures our guides pointed out two which they said had been done by the emperor himself. I suspected the authorship at the time, because they were colored copies of notable paintings, and I knew that the emperor preferred to do something more original than merely copy the work of another. Of course I did not mention my doubts to these officials, but on complimenting the emperor in regard to them, shortly afterwards, he emphatically disclaimed their authorship, and gave me the name of the friend who had copied them. However, it is now a tradition in the palace of Rominten that these two pictures were done by the emperor, and there is little doubt that successive generations of care-takers will receive this tradition, and spread the error amongst all those who visit that interesting house. We may expect before long to see these works re-

A FORESTER

produced in some magazine as evidence of the emperor's taste as an artist. He is, it is true, clever with his pencil, but in a different and more important way than is suggested by his alleged works at his hunting-box.

His study is a room of equal simplicity with the others, so arranged that should he arrive at an hour's notice he would find it ready for work. On the table in front of him stands a little framed photograph of his wife. There is scarcely more than room enough in the apartment for the large table which he always requires for the purpose of spreading out maps and plans. The room is a literary workshop, and no more. Amongst the ornaments, however, I noticed an excellent photograph of the Prince of Wales, his uncle, looking very slim and graceful in the uniform of a Prussian hussar.

Naturally, the most interesting points about the place were the many antlers fastened to the wall as trophies of the chase. The forester told us that hunting here was not such an easy matter as one might suppose; that they often went six days without finding any game, although on the very next day they might kill two. He thought a fair average would be to bag one deer in every four days. The antlers which appeared to be the most numerous belonged to the Damhirsch or Damwildpret; they resemble the big red deer of Europe, but have at the same time a suggestion of the moose in the shovel character of part of their horns. We were shown the hoof of one of these animals, which I measured and found to be thirteen centimetres in breadth, or about four and a half inches. As I said before, the moose is dying out, but an effort is being made to cross it with Norwegian in the hope of reviving the breed.

The emperor, as is well known, is a capital shot, in spite of the fact that he has little more than one arm to do his work with. His rifle is notable in an exceeding length of stock, by which he is able to shoot with his right hand alone. By long practice and natural aptitude he has succeeded in making one almost forget that his left arm is very weak. As a matter of detail, the sportsman may care to know that the favorite rifle for deer in this place is thirteen millimetres calibre, with which eight grammes of powder are used. The trophies that here adorn the walls have a value far above those which decorate the hunting-lodges of most princes, who, when they go out shooting, stand in a favored spot and allow the game to be driven by them, much as one would a drove of sheep or cows. The game here has to be legitimately hunted, and it is this very difficulty in securing a shot that makes Rominten, in the eyes of the emperor, a favorite shooting-ground.

The characteristic Norwegian decoration of

A STALLION

the hunting-lodge is carried out at other points of the forest, notably a bridge which we crossed on our forenoon's journey with the venerable postmaster-forester and his two shaggy Polish ponies. The bridge was of rough-hewn logs resting upon two series of piles, protected up-stream against descending masses of ice, exactly as in the rapid torrents of Norway. Over the bridge is an arch, made by two beams crossing, at each end of which is carved the same draconical design characterizing the gables of the hunting-lodge. This bridge is interesting from the fact that it was built in four days by eighty-five men of the pioneer corps, who marched to this point for this purpose, did their work, and returned.

We parted from Rominten with many regrets, particularly from the rheumatic old forester who had done so much to make our day brimful of pleasant memories of a glorious forest and a unique race of woodcraftsmen.

## ON A RUSSIAN FARM

THE sight of my friend Alsenstorm was very cheering to me, for it was three o'clock in the morning; the train from St. Petersburg had banged me about since the evening before. I was at a small station on the line to Moscow; from the platform I could detect nothing but gloomy infinities of forest and swamp. No one about the place spoke French, English, or German; my passport was in the possession of the police of the capital; I had slipped away without permission, and had not my friend finally appeared, I should have been in awkward plight.

Alsenstorm is of an ancient Scandinavian stock that has been conspicuous in Russian history since the days of Gustavus Adolphus. He had been educated in Moscow; had inherited vast estates near this station; I had made his acquaintance, no matter where, and had run down to get a glimpse of him and his farming.

The trap that conveyed him, or rather that floundered through the mud under him, was the common peasant cart that is found, in different degrees of modification, from Holland to Siberia, and from the Baltic to the Danube or the Caucasus. With a little increase in expenditure it develops into a gentleman's carriage, though in this case it was so heavily incrusted with thick black mud that I could hardly tell whether the wheels had spokes. The heavily bearded peasant who drove sat on a narrow board in front, his feet resting outside the wagon. At the centre was a cushioned bench for two passengers, and behind was ample room for luggage.

Three tough little native mustangs were hitched abreast to this vehicle. They showed much of the quickness that characterizes horses accustomed to pick their own way, and dodged about among the mud-holes as cleverly as our Western ones do.

Alsenstorm is the type of a man that Russia needs to-day more than she ever did before, but which she is persecuting with blind desperation. He is a blue-eyed, light-haired, broad-shouldered, inquiring, enterprising giant. He is a sportsman, and stood before me with his trousers inside a pair of long boots; a much be-pocketed blouse, belted at the waist; a cartridge-belt over his shoulder; a sporting-rifle in his hand; a loose gray military cloak open about his shoulders; a gray felt hat suggestive of our cowboy. The twinkle of his eye, the warm grasp of his hand, the firm way in which he stands squarely on both soles at once, all his attributes, are attractive to me, and I marvelled that he should live in such a neighborhood.

"Glad to see you," said he, in excellent English. " Here is a caviare sandwich, and here a flask of Madeira. Put them inside of you immediately, for we have a long drive before breakfast."

I obeyed.

Alsenstorm read my thoughts as we thumped and bumped through the mud. From my intercourse with him in another country I had been led to expect something better in the way of an estate than what he was inflicting upon me now. There was an awkward silence. He then said to me :

" Since living here, I have become charitable to suicides—I become desperate with the desire to talk honestly and freely." He looked at me a moment with pathetic earnestness, then, in the manner of a man that determines upon a great risk, he said : " I think you are safe. Listen.

" My family is Russian, if two centuries on Russian soil can make it such. Our name has never been absent from the government list of military or civil servants of the czar—our family has served the czar with loyalty. But since the present rule we have become 'suspect,' because our blood is not Slav, our religion is not Greek. My blood remains Scandinavian, my religion is Protestant, and until I renounce my creed I shall continue to be regarded by the priests, the peasants, and the police as one incapable of genuine loyalty to Russian ideas.

"While studying at Moscow I knew that I should inherit the vast landed estate which constitutes all our wealth to-day. For the purpose of fitting myself to take charge of this property I went abroad and studied in Germany the best methods of irrigation, cattle-breeding, engineering, bridge-building, etc. I was fired with the ambition of making my estate a centre of information for the surrounding villages. I adored the czar who had freed the serfs; I looked upon the Russian peasant as a regenerating force, the unspoiled, generous, progressive element that would take advantage of its liberty, would build primary schools, would lift itself into power, and act as a wholesome check upon official corruption and centralized tyranny.

"You see, I knew my peasant only from novels, as some philanthropic Americans knew the negro before your great Civil War. I came to my great estate full of zeal for the rights of man, the dignity of labor. I was determined to show my Russian neighbors that the emancipated serf becomes a self-respecting farmer if treated with consideration.

"Accordingly, my first act was to call the elders of the peasants together, and to tell them that henceforward they were to be treated as free men, and that the last vestige of serfdom was to be abolished. They appeared apathetic, but I believed it to be for their good, and they consented.

"In my father's time, even after 1861, when serfdom was abolished, the peasants all continued their old relations, preferring to work on shares rather than pay rent. With my advanced notions of liberty, this smacked of mediævalism; I wished to pay in money for the day's work of a free man. Consequently, the peasants bought themselves loose. Under the Emancipation Law they received a certain amount of land to work on their own account; the purchase price was advanced to them by government, and was to be repaid out of increased taxes. I received from the state a lump sum for my land, and this money I promptly applied to improvements. Bridges and roads were repaired; I started a brick factory, so that I might have better material for my proposed new buildings; the outlook was splendid; and the crowning happiness was in the thought that henceforth I was to deal, not with serfs, but honest and industrious freemen.

" Early in the spring I had more laborers than I needed, but as the year wore on towards harvest they became lazy, and some of them disappeared. This did not worry me, for I was confident that the great majority were bound to me in gratitude and loyalty. One fine day, however, I was asked to step outside, that the peasants wished to speak with me. I came to the door and said, in my most friendly manner: 'Well, children, what is up?' They behaved respectfully, but I noticed that they had a dogged appearance. 'Please, your honor,' said a black-bearded one, who acted as spokesman, 'we can't work any longer at the present rate; the peasants twenty versts from here are getting twice as much, and we must have the same.'

"In such a case my sense of justice spoke for the peasants. The story they told was a lie, but I did not know it at the time, and in order to show them that they had in me the right kind of an employer, I answered without hesitation:

"'Certainly, children; you shall have as good wages, and I hope you will now work twice as hard.'

"'That we shall!' shouted they, earnestly; but they did not move.

"'Anything more you would like?' asked I, with some irritation.

"Then the long peasant with the black beard spoke for the crowd. 'We cannot go to work unless you pay us half the wages in advance.'

"'Nonsense!' said I. 'You will only go to the rum-shop with it.'

"But they doggedly insisted. I saw my beautiful fields ready for harvest, and recognized the painful dilemma in which I was placed—either pay these dishonest peasants or risk my whole crop. So I paid them the stipulated half, and they went off to work full of zealous promises.

"A short time after this I rode out to the fields and could not see a single harvester. The overseer came to me wringing his hands:

"'My God, my God!' he said; the scoundrels heard of a church festival three hours from here; they have all gone; I can get no one to take their place.'

"I saw that nothing could be done. They had broken their contract, and the law allowed me to sue them. But that would not save my crops! I returned to the house with shaking convictions regarding the value of 'free labor,' and waited a few days until they returned and had recovered from their prolonged spree.

"The next time I met my peasants they were sitting in a ditch, passing a brandy-bottle from mouth to mouth. With difficulty they found their feet. Of course I gave them a strong lecture on their dishonesty, and threatened them with the legal consequences of their breach of contract. This lecture made not the slightest impression; but when I was done, the long black-bearded spokesman again came forward, and told me that it was impossible for them to do any work unless I paid them the other half of their wages in advance. At this I was furious, and rated them soundly; they listened good-naturedly, but, like children, repeated their request—finally saying, flatly, that it was impossible for them to go on with the harvest unless they had their money in advance.

"I was in their power; there was no labor to be had excepting the former serfs; my fine crops were lost unless I could have them immediately harvested. So I once more yielded. They received now their full pay in advance, and for a couple of days worked like happy children. On the third day, however, a large share of them disappeared, and by the end of the week I had not a single one. Half of my crop was left rotting in the field, to be finally buried by the snow.

"Meanwhile I noticed from time to time that planks and beams were missing from my bridges. At first I sought to replace them; but finally gave the matter up, and we now plash through the streams as best we can. The peasants stole the wood for fires rather than bother to cut it for themselves, and had not the slightest interest in keeping the highways open. I tried to catch the thieves, but the peasants hold together like a secret society, and all my efforts failed. I did learn, however, that the peasants who had taken my money and broken their contracts were not far off; so I had the spokesman arrested for the sake of an example, and he was locked up for five days—five happy days to him, for they we passed in complete idleness.

"A week after this came a grain-dealer from Moscow, and I signed a contract for the little crop I had harvested at a fairly good rate. The grain was to be delivered on sleds in two days, and I figured that with the proceeds of this grain I should close the year with only a small loss. As I was figuring, the overseer burst into the room with a shout:

"'The barns are on fire!'

"'It cannot be,' I said, quietly; 'you are mistaken.'

"But I was soon convinced. The guilty one was never brought to trial; no one could be found who knew anything about it. But in the villages every man, woman, and child was telling how the long black-bearded spokesman had taken his revenge."

The story of Alsenstorm I have told because it is a common one all over Northern and Central Russia, and because it explains the "down-at-the-heel" condition of agriculture in the czar's dominions. Had it not been pointed out to me, and explained by competent authority, I should still have suspected that something was very rotten about a system that produced millions of peasants who lived like animals—not animals of much value either, for from the Black Sea to the Gulf of Finland, whether in Bessarabia or Kieff, ovno or Novgorod, Volynien or Poland, wherever I have seen a well-thatched hut, a well-fed cow, a well-dressed mother, or a well-made road, I have usually had to learn that it was owing to exceptional circumstances, or that it was a German or " Kurland " colony.

In Russia nothing is done without violence and police assistance. Nothing develops, nothing ripens, nothing grows from little beginnings. When the czar wanted nobles, he ordered them as he would order a regiment; the social grades of Russia have been regulated by imperial edicts and with no reference to grades above or grades below. The noble was placed above the serf, and so long as the noble held a knout in his hand the serf worked fairly well. Thirty years ago, however, the czar took the knout out of the noble's hand, and told the serf he could do as he pleased. Since that day the condition of the landed proprietor has become steadily worse; but, what is more to the point, the condition of the peasant has not improved. In one county of the province of Moscow, said my friend, out of 208 estates, 188 have been allowed to go to rack and ruin—no cow, no horse, no workmen to be seen. In the same province, out of 298 estates, there are only eighteen on which the owners live the greater part of the year. If this is the case in a province holding the second city of the empire, what can the state of things be in other and less-favored parts? The Russian government gives us no reliable figures from which an economist can draw exact conclusions; but Alsenstorm, who knows what he says, tells me that the state of agriculture in Russia is deplorable, that Moscow is typical of the whole country, and that the present condition of things shows no sign of improvement. To understand Russia, one must go into the hut of the peasant, exactly as one must know the cabin of the negro before discussing politics south of Mason and Dixon's line.

The Russian peasant is worth a diagnosis, for his class represents about nine-tenths of his vast country. Profoundly ignorant and helpless—for reading, writing, and arithmetic are occult sciences to him—he must always lean up against some one else. He knows only what he is told by his priest and equally shallow neighbors, and is infinitely credulous and superstitious. He will believe any smooth-tongued scoundrel who promises him something nice, but is very suspicious of an educated person who encourages him to work and lay aside. Work of any kind he dislikes, particularly if it requires consecutive energy; and agriculture is the kind of work he likes least —his taste is more for trafficking. He has no love for the soil on which he has been raised, is restless, fond of change. His main pleasure is gossip in the tavern over a glass of brandy. He is without moral character, addicted to petty thieving, lies fluently, has no aversion to begging, and is constantly expecting that some happy accident will better his fortunes.

This is the man to whom the future of Russia was intrusted thirty years ago, and history sadly confirms my friend Alsenstorm in stating that the peasant of to-day is, if anything, more devoid of moral character, more shiftless, more drunken, more dishonest, more ragged even than in 1861. The record of elementary education in Russia proves that the peasant cares little for the means of raising himself. He has exchanged masters and made a bad bargain. To-day he is the slave of the man who has advanced him a little money on his crop or his cattle; of the tax-gatherer; and of the village community. The peasant to-day is a pauper; he is constantly in debt, and hounded by creditors more merciless than the most brutal of his former masters. He has not the fuel to warm his house in winter, he huddles his whole family and himself on to the stove at night, and when that does not keep warm he fills his hut with cattle to raise the temperature. His life is as hopeless as that of the dumb brutes he consorts with, and the vodka he drinks gives to him the only paradise he is capable of grasping.

The serfs worked because they were flogged if they did not. Many philanthropists believed they would work harder as free men than as slaves. The knout was abolished; but they stopped working. As serfs the master was bound to see that they had good houses, that they were well clad, that they had proper medical attendance. He punished the idlers, but he had a direct interest in having on his estate only the strong and healthy. Now the sickly peasants rot in their cabins, and no one cares. The harvest fails, and no granaries have been filled. There is no one to insist upon rational methods of agriculture, and consequently the soil is exhausted, and short-sighted selfishness plays havoc on all sides. The landed proprietor, on the other hand, is violently deprived of labor he has counted on in the past, he is left with a large tract of land surrounded by peasants, who lay siege to him as to a declared enemy. The landed proprietor is regarded as one whom every peasant can rob without offending the moral sense of his class, for so great is the gulf between the late serfs and their land-owners that as yet every attempt to identify their interests has failed. The late master, finding his life intolerable in the country, sells his land to estate agents, or disposes of it in any way he can, and, wherever possible, lives in town, or solicits some small salaried post. In this way the only people who have the means and the intelligence to raise agriculture are gradually disappearing from Russian country life, as they have from Ireland, as they have from the Southern States. Their places are taken by shrewd agents, who have no interest but to line their own pockets by squeezing what they can out of the estate and the peasantry round about.

The Russian nobleman never was the ideal farmer, any more than the Russian peasant can be called a good farm-hand. Both have, however, been the victims of such legislation as would probably have harmed the agriculture of any country.

If a German devil had stalked through Russia and scratched his head for the purpose of devising the greatest mischief that could be done her, I fancy he would have hit upon the present system of peasant community. The czar who signed this wicked law meant to do good, but he gave another illustration of the great danger that governments run when they permit the caprice of a philanthropist to override all practical experience of industrial and social development.

The Russian peasant of to-day is something of a Communist or Socialist. He is one of a community owning land in common. In most local matters affecting the little village of one or two hundred souls he has a voice, and the government that affects him most nearly is that of the elders whom he has helped to put in power. Out of the common land he receives a share proportionate to the size of his family, and this share he is supposed to cultivate with public-spirited zeal. Every few years the elders declare a new partition of land, owing to changes in the community caused by deaths, marriages, births, or emigration to other parts of the country. This repartition of land sounds very just, and even practical, to one who has never seen the peasant. As a matter of fact, it is the one feature of modern Russia that makes improvement impossible; for is it likely that you or I would work hard upon a piece of land if next year it were to pass out of our control? Is it reasonable to suppose that an ignorant peasant is going to carefully manure a patch the benefit of which is to be reaped by his neighbor? In the Russian village system the peasant who has done his work well often finds that he has to exchange his field for the neglected one of a neighboring drunkard. Little by little the energy of the most public-spirited evaporates, and each seeks to get what he can from the soil with the least possible expenditure of work. In the days of serfdom there was a master who looked to it that the fields were properly tilled and the soil not exhausted. To-day there is no such check upon the peasant's idleness.

Whoever reads this no doubt says to himself: "But why does not the peasant shake himself free from this stupid community, and buy land and raise himself to the position of an independent farmer?"

Oddly enough, not only does the peasant not do this, but he does not even show the desire to emerge from the slavery of his fellows. The old landlords are only too glad to make easy terms of purchase for any one who will take their acres, but, so far, the only purchasers are speculators and land-sharks from the towns, who traffic in estates with no reference to increasing their values. Occasionally a peasant has shown sufficient energy to get possession of a little patch adjoining that of his "communistic" one, but the village elders eye such a proceeding suspiciously, and his fellows are apt to boycott one who pretends to be better than the rest. If the energetic peasant proposes to manure his property, the elders interfere and order him first to manure the one he holds in common; the village elders exercise an almost absolute control in their community, even to the extent of sending to Siberia any peasant they regard as "unsafe." Nothing in their eyes is so "unsafe" as to show a disposition to rise above the common level of the communistic herd, and such a one they are able to ruin if they bear a grudge against him.

For the government in Russia does not tax the individual peasant; it ignores him completely, and notices only the village elders, who represent a community of about two hundred souls. Their elder chief is responsible to the government for the taxes, and his authority is unquestioned so long as the tax-collector is satisfied. Obviously, the community at large looks with hatred upon any member who expends any part of his energy outside of the community, and many other reasons conspire to force the peasant to remain stuck in the mire, even had he the training, education, and blood of the German. Perhaps of these reasons the most potent is, that no peasant can move from his village without the consent of the elders, and this permission cannot be granted unless the peasant has paid his obligations, both at the village store and the tax-office. The Russian peasant resembles the Southern negro, in that both are quick to seek credit of the usurer, and both averse to settlement, the consequence of which is that the Jew of Alabama or Georgia bears a close resemblance to the village elders of Novgorod or Kieff.

"In spite of what I have suffered at their hands," said Alsenstorm, "I cannot help feeling sorry for these poor Russian peasants. They cling to a communism that has made them little better than wild beasts or paupers; they court ignorance, and are the prey of a besotted priesthood; they have all the faults of children, and scarcely a virtue that we associate with man. Let me tell you something else:

"One fine winter's morning sleigh-bells jingled in our village. A police-captain and his lieutenant made their appearance, wrapped up in furs.

Behind them was a mysterious bundle covered with a cloth. This all happened before I settled here, but the impression is fresh still. The peasants gathered quickly about the strangers, anticipating nothing good from the appearance of a police-officer in their midst. The captain alighted slowly from the sleigh, eyed his audience sharply, while he calculated the amount he could wring from them; then said sternly:

"'Where is your village elder?'

"'Here, your grace,' answered a white-haired, venerable peasant, bowing abjectly.

"'Your name?' continued the police captain.

"'Ivan Ivanovitch, your grace,' answered the old man, bowing again almost to the earth.

"'Ivan Ivanovitch,' said the captain impressively, addressing the congregation of trembling peasants, 'a terrible crime has been committed close to this village on your land.'

"'In God's name, what?' asked the old man, turning pale.

"'See, then, for yourself,' said the police-captain; and with that he threw off the cover and revealed to the panic-stricken gaze of the simple villagers the mutilated body of a dead man. 'This is a frightful crime,' continued the captain, 'and there must be a dreadful retribution. Your community is responsible for this murder, and must bear the consequences. There must be a commission sent here ; the matter must be investigated.'

"'Anything but that!' begged the village elder piteously, stroking and kissing the captain's coat. He knew too well that such a commission meant ruinous fines, to say nothing of floggings for every witness. The peasants with one voice joined in the appeal: 'Anything but a judicial inquiry.'

"' But the matter is very serious,' said the captain ; ' an inquiry must be held.'

"'But perhaps you can help us out of the trouble,' said the elder, persuasively.

"'Perhaps!' mused the captain. 'But it will cost me a lot of money.'

"'What do you want us to pay?' asked the elder.

"'One hundred rubles may do it,' said the captain.

"'One hundred rubles!' screamed the desperate peasants. 'We haven't got so much in the whole place ; you want to ruin us!'

"'Take fifty,' pleaded the venerable elder.

"'What, you rascals! do you take me for a beggar, that you seek to dicker with me? However, you seem to be poor ; I shall insist only on seventy.'

" The peasants agreed sadly to the bargain; the money was paid ; the captain and his lieutenant climbed into the sleigh once more, and drove away with the corpse to the next village. Here they repeated the same performance, and as long as the cold weather lasted that corpse represented at least fifty rubles out of every village community it visited. Of course, that particular trick will not be repeated in our lifetime; but others just as brutal will take its place, for the peasants are always ready to be fooled and fleeced by any one who comes along dressed either as a policeman or a priest.

"Speaking of priests," continued Alsenstorm, "there are priests and priests. Ours are mostly coarse and corrupt, and not essentially different from the peasants they are supposed to elevate. They do not get proper pay from the government, and unless they are industrious and work their land very thoroughly they cannot make a very good show at the end of the year. There are, however, a great many indirect ways in which they make this deficit good, and where their flocks are far from the main line of travel they have many temptations to line their own pockets under the pretence of collecting for their church. Of course they make quite a little trade by funerals, weddings, and the like; and vastly more by blessing cattle and crops, and frightening away devils and plagues. With a peasantry so credulous and helpless as that of Russia, the post of village priest is one of great power and considerable profit.

"Somewhat to the eastward of us is a village where they have what they call *Black Day*. It is not well for me to designate time and place too closely; I only add that this village is inhabited by very poor peasants, who, somehow or other, have slipped away from the gentle ministrations of the Greek Orthodox Church.

## A MISSIONARY TALE

"One fine day, when the sun was shining kindly, the flowers smiling sweetly, and the birds proclaiming the goodness of God, a panting lad rushed into the place shouting '*Black Day!*' The peasants flew from their huts to learn more of the sad news; mothers clutched their babies, fathers clinched their teeth, even little children realized that danger was near.

"'What have you seen?' asked the mothers.

"'A priest with a district inspector in one wagon, and another wagon full of police.'

"A thick cloud of dust appeared between the last houses of the village, and soon the two wagons drew up in the centre of the wretched place. Out jumped the priest; behind him stood the soldiers, one of whom held a rope.

"'Here, you,' said the priest sternly, pointing to the nearest villager, 'show me your certificate of having come to communion?'

"'Dearest father,' answered the peasant, 'I haven't got it.'

"'You dog!' continued the Gospel messenger, 'why did you stay away from communion?'

"'The harvest—hard work—my wife was ill. Oh, forgive me, dear little father!' cried the wretched man. And falling on his knees, he clutched the hem of the priest's robe.

"'I'll teach you to find time,' said the priest, significantly. 'Twenty-five will suit him—eh?' said he, turning to the district inspector, whose military cap, rows of brass buttons, belt, boots, and sword gave a strangely military character to the missionary enterprise.

"The inspector had been a non-commissioned officer in the army, had served in the Turkoman campaign, and understood the Oriental methods of earning money by official means. He and the priest were working this route on joint profits, and there was no danger, therefore, that the secular arm of the law would be raised to shield the crouching heretic from the sentence of the ecclesiastical one.

"The priest's query was answered by an approving nod, and the police servants promptly produced from beneath the second wagon a bench constructed with particular reference to the dimensions of a human body. The peasant was roped down to this with a dexterity born of constant practice, and a police soldier commenced to lay on the blows with a heavy lash. At the ninth blow the back of the priest's victim suggested the meat on a butcher's block, and at the tenth he roared out:

"'Dearest father, have mercy! I will pay what I can!'

"The police-inspector ordered a halt, and the priest asked, gently:

"'Well, what will you pay for your sins, my sweet child?'

"'Five rubles!' groaned the victim.

"'That's a fine joke,' laughed the police-inspector. 'You take us for fools. Ha, ha! only five rubles. Go on with the flogging.' And the hissing lash cut deeper into the peasant's back.

"'You shall have ten!' roared the peasant.

"'Nonsense; go on with the flogging,' answered the police-inspector.

"'Twenty!' finally came from the half-dead body on the butcher's bench.

"The priest leaned his mouth to the poor fellow's ear and said, insinuatingly:

"'Let me intercede for you; make it twenty-five—that is a nice round sum; it breaks my heart to have you suffer. Shall we say twenty-five?'

"The peasant could only nod his head feebly in sign of assent. The soldiers unstrapped him, his shirt was thrown over his bleeding body, and away he staggered to his hovel. The little money he had saved in the hopes of buying a cow, or perhaps paying off arrears of taxes, was taken from him, and put into the pockets of the priest and his official partner. That night was a bitter one in the hut of that poor man and his family. His only crime had been to worship God as he saw fit. He had harmed no man, had violated no law which a civilized man can respect. That poor peasant is too poor to emigrate, too ignorant to change his occupation, too helpless to avoid the petty tyranny that presses upon him. His cries never reach the outer world, for to him *heaven is high and the czar is far away.* No newspaper correspondents penetrate to his miserable corner, and if they did they would never have gone back alive. Priest and police can do there pretty much as they like. No questions will be raised, so long as the government receives the amount of taxes it has reason to expect."

Alsenstorm's story made me feel sick, for it went on to tell me how the clerical beast went on from one peasant to the other, flogging each in turn, until he had squeezed out all the money that could reasonably be expected. Afterwards the cabins were searched in turn for any images or emblems that might be unorthodox, and when the visitation was completed the peasants stared blankly at one another, as people over whom a devastating blizzard has passed. Of course, I suggested to my friend that the case he mentioned must be very exceptional indeed.

"Exceptional!" exclaimed he, excitedly. "I wish it were. The Greek Church, backed by the Third Section, is visiting every village of the empire, in the same spirit, if not with the same instruments, that I have referred to. The Protestants of the Baltic provinces, the Finns, the Poles, the non-conforming Russians in every part of the country, the German colonists in Bessarabia—all are the objects of persecution to the fullest possible extent. The more remote the heretic, the more brutal are the means employed for his conversion. In communities where the people are educated the priests have to be careful, but the spirit that underlies the war-cry of 'Russia for the Russians' is the same that watched the flogging of that bleeding heretic to the eastward of us. The Russian Church improves nothing; it can only drag down, flog, and exterminate. Give it time, and one day we shall lose the little light that still glimmers in Poland and along the Baltic."

At the close of our long drive I was amazed to find a village whose streets were clean, whose houses were substantially built and in good repair. The little children looked as though they had prosperous fathers and mothers—in other words, it did not seem like Russia. The fields I had passed showed good husbandry, the cattle looked strangely sleek; in short, all the signs were such as I thought to have left behind me when I crossed the frontier.

"I meant to give you a shock," said Alsenstorm, "and now I will tell you about it. The people you find about me now are from the Baltic provinces of Kurland and Livland—countries settled originally by Germans; I have attracted them to this wilderness by giving them the opportunity of purchasing a portion of my land on reasonable terms, and spreading payment over many years. They are all peasant-proprietors, these Kurlanders, self-respecting, thrifty, industrious people. Their blood is not German, but their people have enjoyed centuries of German civilization. They are Slav, and would be as dirty and shiftless as their kinspeople of Russia, had they known no other government than that of the drunken elder or the county police. In the land they come from the roads are well-made and maintained; every village has a tidy school-house. The fields are well drained and cultivated; the nobles live upon their estates, and exercise an excellent influence about them, in the administration of justice and the maintenance of local institutions. The people belong mostly to the Lutheran Church, and everywhere you find well-educated clergymen, who do their duty conscientiously, foster liberal education, and cultivate their land thoroughly. The people of these Baltic provinces have been loyal to the czar throughout the two centuries that they have belonged to his empire. They have enjoyed a large measure of local self-government, and it is this that has made them so superior to the rest of Russia. Their towns are centres of commercial and intellectual activity; no schools in Russia compare with those which the Germans maintain there, and the University of Dorpat is far beyond anything dreamed of by a Russian. The people of these provinces were emancipated from serfdom nearly a generation before the Russian edict was promulgated. The czar's government has produced misery and mischief by its measure; the German provinces effected the change so simply and wisely that it has resulted in blessings. The Russian emancipation created a vast gulf between the noble and peasant, which thirty years has only widened. The emancipation along the Baltic has created an excellent class of independent farmers, who regard their interests as identical with those of their former landlords, and who take the liveliest interest in protecting their present system of education and administration against the demoralizing influence of the Russian priest and policeman.

"The Baltic nobles discussed the question of emancipation long and thoroughly in the first half of the century. They deliberately voted the measure as an economic necessity, although there was among them a large party that thought they would be ruined by the transaction. They had, however, to deal in these provinces, not with a peasantry debased by centuries of ignorance and oppression, but with a set of sturdy people who had been gradually raised to a high religious and educational standard. The nobles voted that each estate should alienate the majority of its acreage to such peasants as chose to purchase at a valuation fixed by law, and in payments covering a long series of years. Other arrangements, such as working on shares, were also made. The peasant thus not only became at once a free man, but earned the right to purchase, on reasonable terms, the land on which his family may have thrived for centuries past. That the peasants of Kurland and Livland have availed themselves at all of these practical provisions shows not only that they are intelligent and industrious, but speaks equally well for the good sense of the proprietors who voted the laws. More than half of the land of that country is in the hands of independent farmers, and every year the number increases."

I stopped my friend here to ask him if Kurland and Ireland had anything in common.

" The Irish question is the easiest in the world, if you will only stop agitation and study it practically. The great difficulty in Ireland is, however, that the Roman Catholic peasantry is grossly ignorant, and has quite lost touch with the only men who are in a position to help it—namely, the landed proprietors. So far as I can see, the dispossessed Irish are about as shiftless and helpless as the Russian peasants, and perhaps for the same reason—centuries of neglect and superstitious priestcraft.

"If the peasants you see about me were of German origin you might attribute their prosperity to that fact. But they are not, and that is the interesting feature of the problem. It shows conclusively that the Russian government has degraded and pauperized its own people, and that it will do the same for those of the Baltic provinces, when it succeeds in undoing what German patience has to-day achieved."

"But if the people of the German provinces are so happy at home," I queried, "why do they emigrate to Russia?"

"If I were a Yankee," answered Alsenstorm, with a laugh, "I would answer you with another question—Why does America get her largest emigration from the best-governed and most prosperous countries? Why do Germany and Austro-Hungary send you together nearly 200,000 in one single year—for these are two countries of enormous wealth, and representing a well-administered and prosperous area. Why should they leave their homes and the advanced civilization that surrounds them, and go away to battle with the hardships of a new country? Of course they go to make money; but then, why do not other countries emigrate in the same proportion? How happens it that these two countries send annually to your country more emigrants than Russia, Turkey, and, I might add, the rest of the non-European world, where wages are very much lower, and the lot of man infinitely harder? I say nothing of England and Ireland, for they speak your own language; yet is it not odd that England alone sends to America quite as many emigrants as Russia? Is it that wages are lower in England than in Russia? Of course not. The Russian peasant is too dull, too drunken, to make the necessary effort. The emigrant is the man who has saved something, who is prepared to look ahead, who will work hard to achieve independence. The German emigrates more readily than the Russian, because he is a better-educated and more self-reliant man.

"I am now answering your question. The peasant of the Baltic provinces comes to Russia because the landlords here offer him their acres at vastly more profitable rates than he can secure in Kurland. It proves that land is hard to get in Kurland and comparatively cheap in Russia. It proves further that the Baltic peasant has much pluck and self-reliance, or he would not venture here, among a population that hates him for his creed, hates him for his supposed German affiliations, and finally hates him for getting on in the world. The Russian peasant, in a country where land is sold for almost nominal prices, finds himself crowded out by a strange people, who convert swamps into meadows, and become rich on land which they have always regarded as waste. The Kurlander's farm is an oasis in a desert of Russian retrogression. The Russian landlord prays for his arrival. He knows that every farm prospers when a Kurlander takes charge. But Kurlanders are hard to get. They feel themselves in the enemy's country when their future rests with police and priests of Holy Russia. It is bad enough to battle with the malice and dishonesty of the Russian peasant, but it is a little too much to have the priest and police also on the side of barbarism."

Alsenstorm is making the experiment. He will probably fail in this, as he did in the first, and we shall perhaps soon hear that he and half his colony have been shipped to the salt-mines of Kara for spreading ideas that are dangerous to society. He is at present doing the one thing which the Russian police cannot pardon: he is teaching the people about him to desire something better than they have known before.

# PREACHING THE GOSPEL IN RUSSIA

THE Baltic provinces of Russia extend from the frontier of Prussia almost to St. Petersburg, and belong to Russia by virtue of a compact guaranteeing to the people of that province religious and civil liberty, according to the law which they brought with them from Germany. Peter the Great confirmed this constitution to them, and the Emperor Alexander II. subscribed to it in 1856; the present czar, Alexander II., however, in 1885, repudiated the obligations solemnly entered into by his ancestors, and by this act removed the only barrier protecting this province against persecution by the orthodox clergy. The Russian government had constantly invaded the liberties of their German subjects, but had never questioned them in theory until the present reign. The late czar, in fact, went so far as to rebuke the Greek clergy for their intemperate proselytizing zeal in the Baltic provinces, and in 1865 he issued a secret order to them that they might henceforth stop meddling with Lutheran peasants.

The present czar gave the following answer to

the Protestant people who begged of him only the right to worship God according to the usage of their fathers: " That his majesty had read the petition, and had been pleased to order that such request should never again be made. His majesty hoped that the nobles would do their duty towards the absorption of the Baltic provinces into the rest of Russia, and in this manner show their loyalty. His majesty regarded the Baltic provinces exactly as he did the rest of Russia, and would deal out to them equal justice and also equal law, without any privileges whatever."

This answer meant that from that time forth the Baltic provinces were handed over to the government of the Greek Church and the Russian police, without any reference to solemn promises often renewed. What the present state of things is may be gathered from the story of Dr. Brandt, a Protestant clergyman, at a place called Palzmar, who was dismissed from his post and expelled from the country by the Russian government for the crime of having preached the gospel.

Shortly before the twenty-fifth anniversary of his pastorate, on February 2, 1883, he received from his superiors notice that he had been criminally charged at the bar of the Greek Church for having married peasants who had left the Protestant Church, had gone over to the

Greek, repented, and had now come back to their first preacher. This case was being tried when, in May of 1886, he was brought before the criminal court for the same offence, and also for having confirmed people of his own religious faith. Before this tribunal the pastor was completely acquitted, at least by the reconverted peasants, who insisted that they were Lutherans, had never been anything else, and did not wish to change their faith.

It ought to be explained here that, prior to 1865, about a hundred thousand peasants of the country had been lured into the Greek Church by promises of land and other worldly advantages which, at the time, were particularly effective, as the country had suffered three successive years of bad crops, and, moreover, the Greek priests assured them that there was no difference between Lutherans and orthodox, excepting that the orthodox enjoyed the favor of the czar, and the Lutherans could not be regarded as anything else than disloyal subjects.

To make a long story short, these poor peasants soon found out their mistake—first, that they did not get the land that was promised them, and secondly, that they had changed the ministry of educated and spiritually-minded men for a ritual gorgeous enough in its externals, but as barren of Christian quality as the Llama Temple of Pekin.

Now in Russia an orthodox priest can abuse a Protestant as much as he pleases, and proselytize to his heart's content; but if a Protestant dares address an orthodox on the subject of religion, he commits a crime in the eyes of the law. The Greek priests, therefore, had the field to themselves, in coaxing away Protestant peasants of weak understanding; but not a Protestant clergyman dared, in the pulpit or anywhere else, to explain to his people the difference between the orthodox and the Lutheran system of religion. In spite of this, however, the peasants came flocking back to their former pastors, begging to have their children christened, their brothers and sisters wedded, or their parents laid in the grave, according to the rites of their own religion. But this was against the law, albeit the law ran counter to their ancient constitution. The Protestant peasants might become orthodox, but they could not change back into the Protestant faith, they, or their children, or their children's children. Great was the panic, therefore, when it became clear, from the arrest of Dr. Brandt, that they were forever to be cut off from Protestant communion, on account of a thoughtless step, taken under extraordinary pressure. They commenced to organize, and to devise measures by which they could free themselves from the orthodox yoke.

At about this time, in May of 1885, there arrived a Greek bishop from Riga to this quiet place on a journey of inspection. A crowd of the reconverts gathered about the place, awaiting his arrival, and hoping from him to obtain the permission they so much coveted of once more communing with their own people. The bishop went into the Greek church, and after a short service there came out, and by means of an interpreter invited the people to come in to listen to a service which, he assured them, they would soon learn to enjoy. He said, also, that he would make them a present of books. But the peasants shook their heads, and said they were Lutherans, who had only come to beg the bishop henceforth to consider them as not of the orthodox church. Upon this the bishop told them that they had come there at the instigation of the Lutheran pastor; but this they emphatically denied, assuring their accuser that they came because their conscience troubled them, and they wished to persist as Lutherans. The bishop then took another course, and pointed out that the Greek Church was stronger than the Lutheran, which would soon go to pieces, and that the czar was orthodox, and only through him could any one secure everlasting happiness. He told them that the Lutherans would not be considered at the Judgment Day, but would lie rotting in their graves, whereas the orthodox would rise and go to heaven. A peasant then asked the bishop if any one had ever seen an orthodox rising up to heaven, and another asserted that if they dug up the graves of Lutheran and orthodox they would find that the orthodox were in no better state of preservation than the Lutherans. The bishop then threatened that he would have their Protestant pastor dismissed, and leave them entirely without a church, if they did not behave themselves as orthodox. Whereupon the peasants answered that, even if this took place they would have the Word of God within them, and would no doubt bury one another after a fashion; would form a Lutheran society, and appoint the most learned among them to tender the sacrament.

On the following day came Anne Kursemneeks, a thirty-two-year-old peasant of the place, accompanied by her sponsors. They declared to the bishop that she was baptized a Lutheran, and begged of him a certificate to the effect that the orthodox clergy had no claim upon her. The bishop answered curtly that the Lutheran pastor must have instigated her to this step, otherwise she would not have come, for if she had been baptized a Greek, and entered in the church book as a Greek, she would have to remain orthodox. But she answered that she had come entirely of her own impulse, that she had no idea of ever becoming orthodox, and she only sought this certificate to protect her against claims that were apt to be raised by the orthodox clergy. Hereupon the bishop walked back into his private room, and there presented an eikon, or holy image of the Virgin Mary, telling her to say her prayers to it. But this she declined to do, saying that she recognized only Jesus Christ as intermediary with the Almighty. A priest then urged her to take it, stating that if she did so the bishop would forgive her sins. To this she answered that such forgiveness was beyond his powers, because he was only a man, and that even their pastor never pretended to as much as this, for he only pointed them to God. She was then told that she was a great sinner. This she admitted, but she comforted herself by the reflection that the publican in the Bible was also a sinner and received forgiveness, whereas the Pharisee did not fare so well; "besides," said she, naïvely, "the orthodox priests know nothing of my sins except that my father left the Protestant Church and became orthodox."

She did not mention, by-the-way, that he had allowed himself to be confirmed while in a drunken condition.

They then told her that the czar would have her punished for her obstinacy, but this she answered cheerfully by saying that he might have her life but not her faith. Hereupon the Greek priests ordered her out of the room.

All this seems strangely childish and mediæval

when it appears in print; but as I listened to the recital of this story from a venerable man who had held high office under the Russian government, and who, though used to official heartlessness, could not restrain his tears as he detailed this episode in order to make me appreciate the state of existence in his native country, it made on me an impression which I cannot hope to reproduce among people accustomed to legal safeguards for their constitutional liberty.

When the reconverted peasants found they could do nothing by beseeching the Greek bishop, they turned to the officials of the law and begged them to assist in getting a petition to the czar on this subject; but these authorities would have nothing to do with the matter, remarking that Church affairs was no business of theirs. Even the administrative body of the Lutheran Church, the consistory, declined to receive a petition on this subject signed by one hundred and thirty-six reconverted peasants, that is to say, peasants who wished to return to the Protestant faith, which they had left under circumstances which no one familiar with the matter could reasonably call a change of heart or mind. The reasons for this denial of comfort by the heads of the Protestant Church organization were obvious; for, as we have seen, they exposed themselves to criminal prosecution by taking an attitude which brought them into conflict with the orthodox communion.

In the midst of this religious excitement appeared the czar's order of July 26, 1885, which brushed aside all the mitigating measures which Alexander II. had conceived and published secretly in 1865 (March 19th). The effect of this was to place a strict watch upon every Lutheran preacher, to see that he kept absolutely clear of the reconverted peasants. It also made it a crime for the children of mixed marriages to enter a Lutheran church, no matter what the desires of one or both parents might be. We may imagine the consternation that seized upon the Protestant community when these regulations were, as the law required, read from the pulpit of every church throughout the Baltic provinces, and the doors of the Protestant parsonages were thronged with panic-stricken Lutherans, who begged that something might be done for them to rescue at least their children from the cruel claims of the orthodox priesthood.

Dr. Brandt was regarded as one of the most cautious among the Lutheran clergymen in the Baltic provinces, and those who importuned him he advised to remain quiet, to avoid every appearance of conflict with the constituted authorities, to make no effort towards taking the communion by stealth, and to hope for a change in the law. He believed, as most people did at that time, that the czar could not possibly mean to persecute the unorthodox, and was perhaps acting in ignorance of the true state of things. In this belief he hastened to St. Petersburg, and had an interview with the chairman of the Committee on Petitions, for the purpose of ascertaining if one on this subject would be entertained. The official expressed himself in a hopeful manner, promised to support the Protestant cause before the emperor, and suggested that three petitions only should be submitted, each conceived in a different way, by three different members of the community. With this cheering message the reverend pastor hastened back to his flock, told them the result of his mission, and selected as petitioners three reconverted peasants—by name, Peter Leitis, John Ohsol, and Anne Kursemneeks—who straightway sat down to the momentous task of addressing their dread sovereign, the present czar. It was a dangerous thing to do, and they knew that by this act they were exposing themselves to great risk; but the spirit of martyrs was in them, and they subscribed their names as cheerfully as did the great Reformer four centuries ago. The Russian school-teacher was then called for the purpose of making the translation, for these peasants are not Russian, and know nothing of the Russian language. On the following morning, the 19th of October, this momentous document left the little village of Palzmar, from which it had to journey about forty miles until it reached the railway that joins Riga with St. Petersburg, for Palzmar is about half-way between Pskov and Riga. Many were the fervent prayers offered in that obscure little village of the Baltic provinces as the days passed by, and the answer of their gracious sovereign was eagerly looked for. These were but poor, plain people, begging on their knees, and at the close of this enlightened century, nothing more dangerous than the right of worshipping God according to the custom of their fathers, and of baptizing their children in the faith of their parents. How deep the feeling was that animated these simple peasants is well illustrated by the touching petition signed by Anne Kursemneeks and her sister, and I quote it for its historic value:

"LOFTY AND MOST GRACIOUS MASTER AND CZAR,—We cast ourselves at the feet of Your Majesty in deepest humility. We pray that you will glance at us in our unworthiness and allow one beam of your mercy to shine also upon us. Our father, in an unholy moment, denied his faith through the desire of earthly prosperity, and forgetting the welfare of his soul; this act he has since deeply deplored with contrition and heart-felt sorrow. We pray God to forgive our father his undue haste, and believe it to be all the more our duty to abide in the faith of our dear Lutheran teaching, as only in this faith do we find peace for our hearts and comfort for our spirits.

"But the Russian priests of this place seek to force us with violence into the Russian Church, in spite of the fact that from our babyhood we have been, in every respect, members of the

Lutheran communion. They will not listen to the cries of our sorrowful hearts; they do not allow themselves to be moved by our prayers, but, on the contrary, are threatening us with punishment because we will not break from our Lutheran faith. They seek by this means to rob us of the firm foundation on which our eternal hope is based.

"Pity us, therefore, lofty Master and Czar, and permit us, we entreat you, to remain in the faith of our fathers. For, if Your Majesty should not be pleased to grant this prayer, we should be forced to remain outcast and miserable indeed, without Church, without instruction in the Word of God, without the Holy Communion. For we have covenanted in our hearts and in the face of God that we will never surrender our faith. God has heard this prayer—hear it, oh, hear it also, Lofty Master!

"Looking to your almighty lips for a little word that shall make us happy, we remain,

"Your Majesty's most obedient and submissive servants,

"ANNE KURSEMNEEKS,
"SANNE RUDSIT (her sister).
"Palzmar, 18th October, 1885."

The pastor of Palzmar, Dr. Brandt, had confidently hoped from the benevolent expressions of the St. Petersburg official that these petitions would come before the czar in person, and his hopes were naturally shared by the community of his church. But he little knew the deviousness of official practice in the capital. As events proved, the supplications were handed over to the enemy, that is to say, the authorities of the orthodox church, who promptly called in the assistance of the notorious Third Section of the government—the Political Police—with the result that, on the evening of December 3, 1885, a police-officer arrived in Palzmar, and took up his quarters with the Russian priest. On the following morning commenced a series of inquisitorial sessions, with a view to drawing Dr. Brandt and others within the clutches of the law. For four days witnesses were examined, many reconverts, many orthodox, the elders of the Lutheran community, the teachers, and the local officials.

The police functionary had brought a non-commissioned officer with him who acted as interpreter, being occasionally relieved by the Russian school-master of the village. In the anteroom were stationed the two Russians who taught in the school of the Russian priest, and whose business it was to see that none of the victims were allowed to communicate one with the other. These two were particularly active in assisting the cause of the inquisition by threatening with prison such as insisted that they intended to remain Protestant. Those who came out from the inquisition stated that the Russian teacher did not translate properly, and that the police official entered upon his minutes only the testimony which was prejudicial to the Protestant pastor, excluding much that was in his favor.

The rapidity with which this drum-head court-martial was carried on, particularly on account of a foreign language being used, and a manifest desire to confuse the statements of simple peasants, produced a result anything but that usually associated with impartial inquiry. Two of the petitioners, Ohsol and Leitis, along with a number of other victims, were so thoroughly frightened by the threats of the orthodox inquisitors that they recanted by seeking to place the blame upon their courageous pastor; but the great majority, to their glory be it recorded, protested that they were Protestants, and could not be otherwise; that they had become so of their own free will, without any persuasion on the part of their pastor, and that they would stand by him at any cost.

Anne Kursemneeks set an example that makes her name worthy to rank with the noblest, if, under that head, we include those who have given their life rather than surrender liberty of conscience.

The brutal tribunal before which she was dragged asked how she dared presume to address so exalted a being as the czar! To this she answered, with what we may fairly consider inspired simplicity, that she prayed to God every day of the year, and did not hesitate to ask the Almighty for anything that she desired. For this reason she had considered it right to ask the czar, who pretended to be the representative of God on earth, for a favor which he alone could grant.

She was asked how she dared to sign her petition as "most obedient servant," when all the while she was resisting the czar's orders by holding to the Lutheran Church.

She answered that she was prepared to give up everything to the czar, even her life—

At this point a gendarme interrupted her, sneeringly, and said that nobody cared for her life.

"But," said she, ignoring the brutal interruption, "my faith I cannot give away, for it belongs to God."

Soon after this came the turn of the pastor himself, who was charged by this orthodox police-court with having stirred up the people to petition the bishop of the Greek Church, and, finally, to have been the instigator of the petition to the czar. It is hard to see how either of these acts can be construed into a criminal offence, even by a Russian. This charge was incorporated in a paper containing thirteen questions, all of which were to be answered in eight days, and in the Russian language.

Dr. Brandt was frank in meeting every accusation, and protested emphatically that he had recommended the petition to the czar only because it was the only way open to them in their extremity; that those who sought the Lutheran Church did so entirely of their own conviction, and that he had taken no other share in the preparation of the petitions than to read them over, when submitted to him, for the purpose of seeing that the proper forms and expressions were observed. On the result of these petitions hung the fate not only of themselves, but perhaps of all other Protestants in the Baltic provinces, and it could not be expected that at such a time he, their pastor, should stand aloof, when by his assistance the appeal to his majesty might possibly gain in force of diction. We must bear in mind that the little village of Palzmar did not contain many scholars capable of assisting peasants in the preparation of so courtly a document.

The negroes of Hayti have a proverb which says that "the cockroach is usually wrong when arguing with a chicken," an aphorism which is elaborated in the fable of the wolf and the lamb. Dr. Brandt proved his innocence as completely as could be required by any court of law, but unfortunately his argument was made before judges who were convened not to deliberate, but to convict. In the spring of 1886, about three months from the date of his examination, the czar personally ordered this Protestant pastor to be dismissed from his post, and to be banished to Smolensk, where he was to reside under police supervision. Stripped of formal language, his condemnation was—first to become a beggar, then to be exposed to the fanatical persecution of an orthodox community, added to which was the arbitrary tyranny of the Russian police, who cut off his correspondence, and broke in upon him at any hour of the day or night, under pretence of satisfying themselves that he was not harboring disloyal acquaintances.

The political criminal in Russia, as is well known, is exposed to suffering compared to which the life of a convicted burglar is joyful. The burglar is permitted to employ his talents in a useful way, and one for which he is, to a large degree, fitted. The college professor, the artist, the engineer, the physician, last of all, the clergyman of the gospel, who is sentenced for the crime of having done his duty, is condemned to a life that starves not merely his belly but his mind. The government is charitable in theory, for it allows him seven and a half kopecks (less than two pennies of English money) a day. My reader naturally asks why he does not support himself by work. The Russian police has answered the question by forbidding political criminals to engage in any work for which they may be presumed to be particularly fitted. They may not give instructions in anything, not even the piano. The physician may not practise even as a volunteer in an urgent case, when no Russian doctor is to be had. A deposed clergyman is condemned to a punishment more severe than can be readily imagined, namely, idleness, which gives him time to brood upon his starving state, and balance from day to day the relative merits of suicide or insanity. The exile may have kind friends disposed to send him money from time to time, but he has also a postal censor who does not always hand over the money that comes by mail.

The story of Pastor Brandt is the story of many another worthy man in the Baltic provinces. In fact, I was told in Russia last year that eighty Protestant clergymen were then under trial, and would probably be sent to Siberia. The Rev. Dr. Brandt, so I hear, has since been allowed to leave Smolensk, owing to the intercession of powerful friends, perhaps; but more likely because the Russian government felt that it had selected an unfortunate example for its purpose, one which might excite too much sympathy beyond the Russian border. He was, however, not allowed to go back to the field of his Protestant activity, but given some petty appointment in the interior of the empire, where he could no longer be a menace to orthodox propaganda.

While the present czar was making out the order banishing Dr. Brandt, he made another, striking a still more severe blow at the religion of his Baltic provinces. The imperial treasury has given liberally to the orthodox church for the purpose of missionary work among Protestants in the Baltic provinces, notably for the building of orthodox churches, parsonages, schools, and holy shrines. In this year, however, they went a step further, and gave the orthodox church the right to condemn and appropriate to their purposes any Protestant land they chose. On the other hand, the Protestant Church dares not take a single step either towards building or repairing a church without the special permission of the orthodox bishop. A Protestant congregation recently sought to build a church extension, but were forbidden to do so by the orthodox bishop. Then they petitioned to St. Petersburg, but the minister of the interior answered that they must abide by the decision of the orthodox bishop. Hereupon a deputation of the peasantry appealed to the governor, receiving from him, however, an evasive answer. In their extremity they once more sought St. Petersburg, hoping that, at the feet of the czar, their petition would receive attention. It did, but not according to their hopes, for the first of those who signed it was locked up in the damp and unwholesome dungeons of the famous prison-fortress named after Peter and Paul, and there he is to this day, so far as I have any information.

   This little episode is well capped by the fact that, soon after the suppression of a Protestant extension here, an orthodox church was built, although in the whole community there were but seven Russian communicants. In this way, by forbidding Protestant congregations to build churches for themselves and holding orthodox churches near at hand, empty and ready for service, the czar hopes to weaken the cause of the heretics and popularize Panslavism.

The banishment of Dr. Brandt was soon followed by the dismissal of the village clerk, or notary, Carl Semel, and the imprisonment of the village school-master and deacon, Jacob Abel; thus fulfilling the threat of the Russian priest of the village, who said that he regarded these three as the props of German ways of thinking in that neighborhood, and that he would soon make an end of them all. The poor deacon, who was as innocent as his pastor, was condemned as one whose guilt corresponded with that of the Nihilists. He was described as " a politically unsafe man," and it was ordered that he should never again be appointed as school-teacher or as church assistant of any kind. In the spring of 1886 policemen appeared at his door and took him away to Riga, where he was locked up for several weeks as a " political criminal " in the common prison; and when they let him go, in August of that year, it was to send him out in the world little better than a tramp upon the highway; and this was in spite of the fact that he was proved innocent of all charges brought against him. The little village of Palzmar has now two Russian policemen stationed there, who assist the Russian priest in the development of orthodoxy, and as many arrests, examinations, and dismissals from office have occurred since the banishment of Dr. Brandt, it is safe to say that Russification has set in there with a vengeance.

Through the kindness of a trusted Russian friend I have been able to procure some details in regard to another victim of Russian persecution, Dr. W. Harff, who was banished, treated as a Nihilist, kept under police supervision, reduced to beggary, and finally saved through the kindness of German friends, who secured for him a small post in Brunswick. Dr Harff was called to the pastorate of a church in the Baltic provinces, on the river Duna, in 1881; it was a Lithuanian community, with four thousand five hundred Protestant communicants, of whom one hundred were Germans, and was a fairly representative parish. In 1885 he lost his wife at the birth of his youngest son. He had eight children, the oldest of whom was fifteen years, but he was living comfortably, according to the circumstances of the neighborhood, cultivating his little farm and garden, and thus eking out the income which his church allowed him. To use this clergyman's own words: " In the fall of 1887 fell the two hundredth anniversary of the Lutheran Church in our neighboring parish, and we proposed to celebrate the occasion suitably. ' A collection had been made among the proprietors and peasants of the neighborhood in order to restore the church and complete the tower. It was proposed to have the service first in Lithuanian and then in the German language, and, in spite of protests on my part, I was selected to hold the Lithuanian service. I chose my text from the 32d chapter of Deuteronomy, using the words in the song of Moses, 'Ascribe ye greatness unto our God alone.'

"Mindful of the great sacrifices which had been made for the adorning of our house of worship, and the great joy in the hearts of all those partaking in this festive ceremony, I referred, in the opening words of my discourse, to the uncertainties of the present time, the fact that the schools had been taken away from our control, that the building of churches had come to depend upon the permission of the Russian bishop, and that we must prepare to suffer persecution on account of our faith. On this account I urged we should prize all the more the happiness we enjoyed at that moment. What I said dealt alone with facts, but I had said too much to please those whose purpose was to exterminate this land and people.

"Immediately after the service I learned that secret police had been present and made notes. There followed soon secret examinations of many communicants, for this was a common event in those days, particularly with the assistance of fair promises or terrible threats. Four weeks afterwards I was called before a captain of police, who spoke very imperfect German, and who had as his assistant a lawyer's clerk in a striking uniform. They demanded of me that I should explain my conduct in stirring up the people against the recent measures of the government. This it was against my instructions to do, for, according to the last imperial order, no examination of a clergyman should take place unless there were present some one to represent the Church administration. Accordingly I was released, although not before I had been compelled to sign a paper engaging myself not to leave the parish that is, not to escape from the Russian authority.

"For a whole year the matter lay in abeyance; apparently I was free, although actually under observance. In the summer of 1888 I heard that two of my colleagues had been severely punished, but I still tried to comfort myself with the reflection that they could not possibly construe my conduct as criminal. In September of 1888, however, a police official came to my house and announced to me that his majesty, on the recommendation of his minister, had banished me for two years, and in ten days I must start."

The punishment was originally to have been Siberia, but this order was changed for deportation to an interior town of Russia. His colleague of the next parish being exiled at the same time.

Dr. Harff thanks God, from paragraph to paragraph in his pathetic account, for the mercies strewn in his path from the moment of receiving the czar's cruel order. His many children were provided for by charitable neighbors, and one of his relatives took charge of his little farm and garden for him. In order to avoid the demonstration which his parishioners would have made upon his departure, he drove secretly to a remote station of the railway, and there, under the eyes of the police, boarded the train, and left behind everything that was near and dear to him.

In the principal town of the province to which he was banished he had first to report himself to the commander of the police, who proved to be a kindly and cultivated Russian, who did everything in his power to make the clergyman's lot tolerable. It was an immense relief to find that they would be allowed to live where they chose, for they dreaded an order forcing them to live in some filthy village, far from every intercourse with their fellow-men.

Another blessing came to them in the shape of warm friends, who received them into their house, and kept them for the two years of their exile. The case of the Rev. Dr. Harff is, therefore, that of a man whose lot was sweetened to him by everything that could possibly happen in his favor. It is not likely that another clergyman would have met with so many fortunate circumstances while serving a sentence calculated to crush the average man of education. We can easily imagine him to have come under the control of a provincial governor who would have found the height of satisfaction in annoying a gentleman; who would have ordered him to some pestiferous swamp, where the Russian priest and the tax-gatherer would have been at once his jailers and companions. It is not to be supposed that every banished clergyman found himself in a position to leave eight children among good friends, or to have his little estate well managed in his absence. We must bear in mind, therefore, that the case of Dr. Harff is exceptional.

The government, in the case of this gentleman, made no provision whatever for his support. He was, soon after his audience with the governor, called before the police and put through a severe catechism in regard to all his friends and relatives—in fact, the usual questions put to Nihilists when it is sought to trace all their connections and correspondence. The object of this catechism was, of course, to set spies upon those with whom he sought to hold communication, in the hope of having them also tangled up in the police mesh. They gave him also the rule that was to govern his conduct. In a word, he was to live thoroughly retired and quiet, to avoid receiving company, and raise his voice while speaking, never whisper. The police, of course, had the right to make domiciliary visits by night or day, and all the letters of this victim were, naturally, examined. On one occasion a German friend happened to pass through the town, where he remained only twelve hours. Dr. Harff naturally took pleasure in acting as his guide about the place, but had forgotten that political criminals are not allowed to frequent public places. For this violation of the rules he was taken sharply to task by the local police, who had, of course, heard that a German stranger, consequently a suspicious personage, had been seen in company with a deposed Lutheran clergyman.

Early in 1889 a hard blow was struck at our friend, for his majesty then decreed what amounted to an additional penalty, namely, that he should never again be allowed to hold a position in his own country, that is to say, in the Baltic provinces. By this simple decree there was nothing for this political exile to look forward to in the future except beggary and the lot of a man without a country. The saddest feature of these two years was, according to this minister of the gospel, the separation from his family at Christmas-time and on birthdays. One must have lived in Germany to understand the affection with which those anniversaries are there regarded.

At last came the day of deliverance; Dr. Harff was called to the police-station, and there told that he was free. He was about to express his joy, when the officials checked him by ordering him to sign a paper in which he covenanted never to appear in either St. Petersburg or Moscow or the provinces in which they lie. So here was a man of intellectual training forbidden to return to his pulpit, and excluded from the two chief cities of the empire, where he might possibly have gained a livelihood in some occupation for which he was, in a measure, fitted. He now prepared to leave the town where he had spent his years of unhappiness, but such is the tortuousness of Russian officialism that he could not move without a pass, and was forced to wait a full four weeks before this document was furnished to him. With a heavy heart he at last reached the Baltic hamlet, where his children awaited him, and heard from the lips of his neighbors of the many who had died, and the still greater number who were living in daily fear of the police and the Russian priest. No one felt safe; each one dreaded fresh steps in the direction of Russification, which meant the extermination of everything they held dear. Two of his sisters had died while he was in exile, and he began to feel that a place by their side would be the pleasantest rest he could hope for. He had no means of support, and but for the charity of his former parishioners, he would have been reduced to pounding stone by the wayside. Under the political system of Russia there was to him at that time a choice of only two hopes: the one, a possible appointment in Germany; the other, emigration to America. In this final extremity, God, he tells us, answered his prayers; for, in Berlin, some good friends managed to secure for him a small church with at least enough salary to keep him alive and allow him to have his dear children about him.

If we may look at such a time for a silver lining to the dark cloud overhanging the Baltic provinces, it is to be noted that the persecution which has raged in Protestant Russia since the accession of the present czar is likely to enlarge the sympathy of these people for their fellow-victims in Poland, where the Roman Catholics have for many years suffered quite as severely, to say nothing of many Greek Church sectarians who are equally the objects of orthodox malevolence. Shortly after Mr. Remington and I left Russia, a friend furnished me with the following particulars illustrating the manner in which the Greek Church was carrying on its Russifying campaign in Lithuania and Poland: On the 15th of August, 1892, in the little town of Sledzianov, in the department of Grodno, which is a point somewhere between Riga and Warsaw, a large crowd of Roman Catholics and Greek Church sectarians gathered together from remote parts of the neighborhood. They had come to protest their loyalty to the faith of their fathers. There was a church at this point, but the pastor had been deposed, and it had been closed by the police. In some mysterious way the door was found open when the people arrived, and although they had no priest they began a solemn service, even to the extent of taking the holy sacrament, some scraps of bread having been found upon the altar, evidently left there through the carelessness of the officiating deacon. Hymns and fervent prayers filled the church, while round about as many as twelve thousand worshippers gathered who were unable to crowd into the already overfilled building.

The Russian bishop soon got wind of this act of religious insubordination, and ordered his representative immediately to the spot, with whom went the governor, a police committee of inquiry, and a regiment of dragoons. The people were ordered out of the church, but declined to come. They were then told that the building would be set on fire, which threat was partially carried out when the wretched worshippers, exhausted by the fumes of smoke, issued from their sacred building. These were then taken in charge by the cavalry soldiers, who struck them indiscriminately, and treated them as common malefactors. Those whom they chose to select as ringleaders were then, in the presence of women and children, mothers and sisters, stripped and flogged till the blood ran down their backs, and until some of them, at least, died under the lash. In order that the effect of these measures should not be lost upon this rebellious community, the soldiers made a cordon about the place so that all should be witnesses of the brutal punishment, and take warning by the fate of their fellows. When enough had been flogged to satisfy the Russifying committee the peasants were dismissed, and soon afterwards the inevitable police investigation commenced. Many of the peasants were summoned to Bielsk, where they were kept locked up until the government had made up its mind what should be done in regard to the whole matter.

There appears to have been considerable system in this particular government movement, for from Sledzianov the committee with the governor marched off to a neighboring place where there was an equally large Roman Catholic and schismatic community whose church had no pastor or priest. In order to be quite sure that the pious rebels in Sledzianov should not return to their wicked ways, they quartered the dragoon regiment upon them for three weeks, during which time the peasants had of course to furnish all that was needful to their comfort, under pain of having their houses burned down. Their duty it was to patrol the neighborhood, and to harry the villages in which were any heretics, and, it is needless to add, they did pretty much what they chose, as long as their victims were enemies of the Russian priest. The poor people who are being ruined by this system of persecution wonder that the czar allows it, because, as they say, God is obviously on their side, for he has cursed the Russians first with famine, and next with cholera; whereas in Poland, Lithuania, and the Baltic provinces, the harvest has been excellent, and the public health equally so.

The Russifying committee found a vigorous resistance at the next church also, but this was speedily overcome by the strong force of police which was placed at their disposal.

The police committee next marched upon a place called Semyatitch, all in the same general neighborhood, where a Roman Catholic church stood which had been closed by order of the orthodox authorities as recently as the year 1892. The priest had been led away by the police, his house confiscated, all his devotional books likewise done away with, and the very church locked and sealed. As in Sledzianov, however, under the same impulse, the church had been opened again early in the morning, and the people united there in saying their prayers and doing other acts of devotion. The crowd here was as great as elsewhere, for the neighborhood soon got wind of what had happened; but here, as elsewhere along the western frontier of Russia, there is always a convenient regiment of cavalry, and this body was called into requisition by the police. The soldiers were ordered to clear the church, but the unarmed peasantry resisted by locking arms around the church-yard and offering their helpless bodies as a resisting wall to the sabres of their Russian conquerors. The soldiers attacked these people with cold steel, and were answered by a few stones from a distance. One blow led to another, and soon about the sacred premises was a hand-to-hand battle, armed men with helpless peasants—a conflict so unequal as to soon terminate. Here, as in Sledzianov, when the power of the soldiers had been asserted, a number of peasants was selected, and in the presence of their relatives stripped and flogged with Cossack whips until the police judged that their spirit was sufficiently crushed to render them in future submissive and loyal.

The police made a strong effort to arrest those who were suspected of opening the doors of the church. Whether they got the right ones or not is not known, but they have arrested some, and these will probably never see their home or any of their friends again, excepting in Siberia.

Unfortunately for the cause of liberty, the Germans of the Baltic provinces, the Lithuanians, and the Poles hate one another almost as bitterly as each, individually, dreads the process of Russification. They are carefully isolated one from the other by a system of press censorship and police quarantine, so that co-operation between Warsaw, Kovno, and Riga is almost physically impossible, even assuming that the three races here represented could be brought to merge their religious differences for the sake of taking common action against the all-absorbing orthodoxy. These three suffering parties are separated not merely by race and religion, but, beyond that, are so completely overrun by officials, police, and soldiers, that not a letter can be sent, not a meeting held, not a newspaper put into type, without imminent risk of imprisonment or banishment. Two friends I have in Russia dare not send me the most innocent communications for fear of being therefor called to account by the secret police, and when by good-fortune I do hear anything from Russia, I notice that the letter is always posted in Germany, having been first taken across the frontier by safe hands.

One would suppose that the persecution now going on in Russia would rouse the people of

Germany—Protestants and Catholics alike—to such a storm of indignation as would result in mass-meetings and demonstrations. Yet Germans, so far, have been rather apathetic, owing to the difficulty of securing reliable information from their fellow-countrymen in Russia, but principally from the policy of Prince Bismarck, who when in power never failed to show his subserviency to Russia, and indifference to the fate of his coreligionists on the Baltic. Of the Poles he never spoke without contempt, and considered that the sooner they were extinguished the better for all concerned.

Last summer a German official who had been for many years stationed on the Vistula, at the fortress of Thorn, close to the Polish frontier, told me that Bismarck when in power always seconded the Russian police when they claimed any fugitives from Russian so-called justice. Many of these poor political refugees, anticipating arrest, floated down the Vistula from Warsaw, and imagined that in a constitutional country like Germany they would find at least a fair trial. Bismarck, however, as foreign minister, seized such poor wretches on the ground that they were dangerous to the peace of Germany, and must be expelled. Of course he might have expelled them on the French, Swiss, Dutch, or Danish frontiers, but with a casuistry cruel in its refinement he ordered them to be taken to the Russian frontier, where the czar's police received them. Under the present government of Caprivi there has been no disposition manifested of pursuing this brutal policy, and it is to be hoped that the annals of German administration will never again be stained by measures so mediæval and heartless as those which were too common in the days of the Iron Chancellor.

To explain Bismarck's hatred of the Poles, one must understand his dread of revolution, for he cannot imagine a people governed otherwise than by violence. To him there is no man so dangerous as one who thinks for himself, or who organizes to redress a grievance. In the early part of November, 1892, Bismarck said of himself that he once strongly urged upon the emperors of both Germany and Russia to hold together in a firm alliance because "in the interests of monarchy they had more to gain in combating revolution than by separating for purposes of conquest." Bismarck is one of those great men who forget nothing and learn nothing. He remembers that Prussia joined with Russia in partitioning Poland and in suppressing the struggles for liberty in that country. He saw that through overwhelming numbers successive rebellions were put down, and he fancied that peace secured at such a price could be enduring. He has not learned the secret of conservatism in a people as it exists in the United States, in

England, in Scandinavia, in Australia, Canada, and other free countries. In his own country he had been twenty years fighting Socialism by means of suppression, and yet was too blind to see that these brutal measures only made Socialism more dangerous. He does not seem to see the enormous sacrifices which the Poles have made for the last hundred years for their independence, and, above all, their liberty of conscience. In the interview from which I quote he says: " The enemies of peace with Germany are, in Russia, only the Jews, and particularly the Poles. The Poles are cleverer, more cultivated, and have more tact than the Russians; they are masters of conspiracy and deception. . . . They pretend to be friendly with us at present, because they wish us to conquer Russia and restore to them their country," and so on.

For thirty years Bismarck has carefully poisoned the mind of Germans against Poland by pretending that the people of that country were conspiring all the time against monarchy and against society. Had the press of Germany been free during all these years, there would have been papers prepared to refute indignantly this charge against a noble people; but in the absence of contradiction, stories against Poland were published over and over again, until the present generation has almost as imperfect an idea of that country as France has of Germany. Prussians have fought three wars against Poland within a hundred years, and in war time, needless to say, the conquering army does not see the most lovely qualities among the people whose country they are invading. The Protestant Lithuanians and Germans of the Baltic provinces are only now beginning to feel sympathy for Poland; now that both are so miserable that they have memory for nothing but their common wrongs. In the days of their prosperity the Baltic Germans were very loyal to the czar, and sternly set their face against Polish rebellion. Their liberties were so well founded, they thought, and their prosperity so great, that they dared not jeopardize the one or the other by appearing to feel sympathy for the czar's enemies. Little did they dream, in the reign of Alexander II., that in a few short years Russian priests would be forbidding the erection of Protestant chapels, imprisoning their pastors and school-teachers, and sending to jail their most moderate and cultivated men, for simply protesting against the violation of their constitution. The Russian czar is bent upon war, or at least is pursuing a policy which can only end with this result—either civil war or foreign, perhaps both. It may seem strange that God permits in our day religious persecution that would have disgraced the age of Philip II. or Bloody Mary; but perhaps it is only through such an ordeal as this that the victims who are now groaning under the Russian yoke can be brought to recognize the duties which one Christian owes to another, to forget the many savage disputes that have marred the relations of Poles and Germans, and to merge minor religious differences in the great struggle for constitutional liberty. The great lesson of tolerance is sadly needed in Poland and in the Baltic provinces as well as in St. Petersburg; and it may be in the scheme of the Almighty to bring about a better feeling between the two great branches of Christians by a co-operation of Catholics and Protestants, standing shoulder to shoulder in Christian brotherhood, over against a Church whose high-priest is the czar, and whose purpose is to make of Europe a Russian province.

# RUSSIFICATION

#### THE POLISH AND THE GERMAN CHAPTER

AT half-past four of a chilly, misty morning, on the banks of the muddy Memel, without breakfast—is it strange that we should have been cross? We were in Kovno, the much-bespied Russian fortress; Remington\* was making a surreptitious sketch at the head of the long bridge of boats, over which Napoleon's army must have crossed in June of 1812. In fact, we thought we could distinguish the very hill on which the conqueror stood when, in person, he directed the operations of his great army. There was nothing very wrong in sketching a hill associated with the presence of Napoleon I., but I happened to know that, in a semicircle to the south of where we stood, on the opposite side of this muddy stream, the czar was putting finishing touches to a chain of seven forts, the line of which is about three miles distant from the centre of the town. I happened also to know that, in the previous week, two Germans had

\* Frederic Remington, the artist.

been arrested for inadvertently trespassing on fortress ground, and that Russians make scant distinctions between accident and design in the case of people caught wandering about powder-magazines and embrasures. Under the circumstances, neither of us had the slightest desire to push our investigations beyond reasonable limits —we both longed to get out of Russia as quickly as possible.

Kovno has a monument on which is written: " Russia was invaded in 1812 by an army of 700,000 men. That army went back with 70,000." The preparations now making to receive another enemy indicate that Russia does not mean Germans or Austrians to enter beyond this river. In 1812 Napoleon advanced until mud and hunger compelled him to give up. This time Russia means to meet her enemy on a line of forts stretching from the Baltic to the Black Sea. They may be roughly outlined as commencing at Riga and ending at the mouth of the Danube. Those who imagine that Russia will once more retire and draw her enemy into the interior are vastly mistaken, for in that case why spend enormous sums upon fortresses on the western frontier? Why make of Kovno another Metz?

As I rolled this in my mind, I lifted from my shoulder the masts and sails of my canoe, and tossed the clumsy load upon what I took to be a pile of corn sacks covered with tarpaulin. To my amazement a short, sharp scream came from beneath the canvas—a woman's voice, I thought. At such an hour and under such circumstances my curiosity was roused, particularly as the creature beneath did not stir, and the sound was not repeated. Not a soul, not even a policeman, was about; so I raised a corner of the covering, and discovered the crouching form of a frightened mother, hugging a little child to her breast. Remington was absorbed in his illegitimate thumb-nail work, and apparently had not noticed the episode. I was about apolgizing for my clumsiness, when the little mother, in an agitated manner, said:

"Indeed, sir, I have done nothing. I have my ticket. I am waiting for my uncle."

It was pitiful to notice her distress of manner, the evidence of having been hunted by human blood-hounds. Of course I told her immediately that she quite mistook my calling. I was not a detective—merely an American traveller trying to get out of the country with the least possible delay. The hunted look did not disappear, for she was still in Russia—in fact, in the military department of Vilna, amid a garrison of 100,000 men. But she seemed to feel that I, at least, would do her no harm. She was at first shy of Remington, but in time I made her believe that he, too, feared a howling Apache less than he did the most shrinking of women.

We were friends in misery, and, as I mention no names, I may add that she was pretty in spite of the bedraggled appearance of her hair and skirts.

"But what in the world brings you to spend the night in the mud on the river-bank under a dirty tarpaulin?" I asked.

This question made her again shy; but she was by this time partaking of my bread and sausage, and soon concluded to take me into her confidence.

"My husband," said she, "is off in the town with the Jews. He has no pass. He is going to cross the frontier to-night."

"Yes, but what about you and the little one?"

"Oh! I am waiting for some one—there is a raft coming down the river, the captain of which has promised to take me on board and carry me to Tilsit. He is an honest man—a German; I must not go with my husband across the frontier —I could not help him, and might lose my baby"—with which words she kissed the little one, sleeping sweetly at her breast.

Of course by this time I was wrought up to a high fever of romantic anticipation, and wished to ask all manner of questions, but just then the expected raft hove in sight through the river mist; almost simultaneously a long and narrow dug-out canoe ran its nose ashore at our feet; a strong, bearded man plied a stern-paddle, and in a few seconds mother and child disappeared out upon the swift stream of the muddy river.

It was lucky for the two that they disappeared as they did, for the morning was wearing along rapidly, and soon the bridge of boats became animated with peasants and also soldiers. Uniforms seemed to spring from every street opening, and we began to feel as though Kovno was little more than a very dirty barrack. I should not, however, forget to mention the Jews, who also wear uniforms, by-the-way, and who number 25,000 out of a total population of barely 50,000.

Soon, however, a little flat-bottomed Russian steamer paddled away with us down the river, and I watched my fellow-passengers narrowly. Of course there were several uniforms, many Jews and peasants, and a few whom I could not quite make out. Among these an intelligent-looking man of about thirty happened to sit near me, as I sipped a cup of coffee, and from him I sought information. His answers were polite, his manner rather reserved — until, by an accident, he gathered that I was an American, when he admitted that he was a Pole, and commenced to talk freely. He was not, however, quite sure of me until I mentioned one or two of my friends at Warsaw, whom he regarded as leaders of his national party. Then he confessed to me that he was trying to get into Germany that night.

"Then," said I, "I have the honor of knowing

your wife!" With which, to his great relief, I related her successful departure from the Kovno river-bank, in charge of the black-bearded boatman. "But why do you smuggle yourself out of the country?" I asked. "Could you not have accompanied your wife?"

He smiled bitterly, and answered:

"She can be smuggled more easily than I can, for she is a woman. I may escape to-night, if the police are stupid enough, but at any point of this river I am liable to seizure by any official clever enough to recognize me."

"You don't look like a criminal," said I.

"No, but worse than that, I am a Pole, and my country is being 'Russified.'"

I had nothing to say to this.

He paused a moment, passed his hand across his eyes wearily, looked at me fixedly, and then commenced again:

"My father, along with every respectable man in the country, fought for Polish independence in 1863. We gave the Russians a hard fight for it, but finally, with the assistance of Prussia and Bismarck, they got us down and began to kick the life out of us. My father was killed by a Cossack—a handsome young man he was. Of course I was only a baby then, but my mother brought me up to honor his memory and be loyal to my country, my religion, and my mother-tongue.

"Well, our estates were confiscated; my mother struggled along for a time upon the little ready money she had saved, but died of a broken heart in a few years. I was dismissed from the scientific school in Warsaw because some Russian sneak told the teacher that I talked Polish in forbidden hours. Of course I should have been more careful, but they probably would have refused me a degree anyhow, as any excuse is found good enough when the object is to turn out a Pole and put in a Russian—at least, in Warsaw.

"My dismissal made it impossible for me to complete my education anywhere in Russia, and I had not the means to go abroad for the purpose. Money I had very little, so I became a machinist, and by keeping my mouth shut finally secured a pretty good position in one of the mills at Lodz.

"Do you know much about Lodz?" he asked.

I had to admit that Lodz had been to me but the name of a manufacturing town of Poland, and that I had never been nearer to it than Skernevitze.

"Well," said he, "it has about 120,000 people, nearly all of whom work in the factories there. It lies between Warsaw and the German frontier, and in the track of an army invading from the west. Although so important a centre of manufacture, the government does not connect it with the railway system of Europe, but allows it to trade only to the eastward—that is what we call Russian protection. You may measure the importance of Lodz when I tell you that the woollen-mill in which I was a superintendent employed 8000 hands!

"Well, the police have always kept a sharp eye on Lodz because it is so close to the frontier, and because it contains so many intelligent workmen of Polish and German antecedents. It was felt that, in the event of war, the town would organize a welcome to the German emperor, and be an important base for the manufacture of contraband material. The Russian governor at Warsaw, General Gurko, did everything a brutal soldier could think of, therefore, to discourage any but orthodox Russian appointments in our neighborhood. The police had most ample powers to arrest and transport any one suspected of unorthodox views—in fact, to-day not a man can get an appointment or promotion of any kind without police permission. By dint of persistent and judicious bribing, we had jogged along well enough; but on the 1st of May [1892] the operatives had arranged for a labor-day celebration. That was unfortunate, particularly as they concluded to strike on the 2d for a day's work of ten hours."

I objected that I could see no reason why men should not strike for any wages they pleased, so long as they did not violate the law.

"You misunderstand me," rejoined my Polish companion; "I was thinking of the military situation. Lodz, though a mere industrial town, has for its protection a brigade of field artillery, a battery of horse artillery, a regiment of infantry; Cossacks and dragoons to an indefinite extent, within a few hours' ride, and is shut up in a military department that keeps 130,000 men under arms ready to march at short notice. General Gurko enjoys shooting Poles and Turks equally, and to give him any excuse for sending troops to Lodz was unfortunate."

"But why have I heard nothing of all this?" asked I.

"Because General Gurko does not edit newspapers for the benefit of the unorthodox," answered he, smiling. "No Polish or Russian paper has ventured to discuss the matter, and if you ever see anything about it, you may be sure that it was smuggled across the frontier by the Jews. But, as I was saying, the strike commenced on the 2d of May. The men behaved well enough, and it seemed to me that the matter would be amicably arranged by a fair compromise. But General Gurko had evidently other ideas, and telegraphed from Warsaw that the employers should not yield anything. He then marched a column of Cossacks upon the place, and gave the military authorities telegraphic orders not to be afraid of using ball-cartridges.

These items of intelligence somehow or other leaked out among the men, and converted what was originally but a domestic difference into a war against the common enemy. Germans and Poles were smarting under the indignities they had suffered at Russian hands; the troops quartered about them were not Polish — on the contrary, they were men brought from Russian orthodox neighborhoods, and animated with fanatical hatred against the people among whom they were quartered.

"You ask, perhaps, where are our brothers, now serving in the czar's army? Anywhere but in Poland. Some along the Volga, some in the Caucasus, some in Turkestan — but always far away, beyond the cry of their wretched fellow-countrymen.

"The strike soon became serious, and it seems to me that the government intended to provoke the trouble that ensued. They employed police agents who pretended to be working-men, and sought to inflame the mob against the Jews; but this did not work; they were prepared for it. Afterwards, by a strange accident, the inmates of an adjacent penal colony were turned loose in the town and commenced plundering. Meantime the popular feeling against the troops grew to such a pitch that, when a squadron of Cossacks was ordered to charge, they were met by desperate civilians armed with nothing more effective than pocket-knives. The soldiers dashed in among the mass of men, women, and children, but rage seemed to have made us all forget the sense of fear. While Cossacks used sabres and revolvers, the strikers answered by stabbing with their knives until overpowered. It was sad to see the noble horses fall, but I felt little pity for the men who rode them. Eighty soldiers were killed in that week, and two hundred wounded—how many of the towns-people I cannot say, but many times as many, I am sure, for the strike lasted a week.

"The government did what was possible to provoke disorder, and then took advantage of it to set the soldiers on us. It is an old trick in Russia, and always serves its purposes. This time the troops and police had more to do than usual, but the end was clearly foreseen. As soon as the smoke had cleared away, houses were searched and arrests were made wholesale. All foreigners were promptly expelled, and about three hundred Germans escorted to the frontier. Being the son of a Polish patriot, I was arrested as a matter of course, and condemned by a drum-head court-martial to Siberia, along with a hundred or so of my compatriots. It so happened that I had taken no part in the labor demonstration beyond being in the streets in the interest of my factory. No investigation was made of my case, but it was assumed that I had better leave Lodz, and therefore I was condemned. My wife was, of course, nearly distracted, for our child is only about a year old, and banishment to Siberia meant for her a punishment more severe than death.

"But Russian tyranny is marvellously tempered for those who have ready money. My wife had some savings at home, and a Jew horse-dealer did the rest. One night, as the prisoners were whispering together over the intending tramp to Siberia, the jailer came in, touched my shoulder, and said I was to follow him. We passed into a room where we were alone. He handed me a letter from my wife, saying that I should do as I was told, and trust the man who drove me. The words were ambiguous, but I was satisfied. My eyes were blindfolded, my arm seized, and I was marched out of doors. The way seemed long, and not a word was exchanged. At length we stopped, I heard some whispering, some paper money crumpled, my arm was seized by a second person, the jailer's steps were heard retiring. Then my bandage was at length removed, but it was too dark to see anything. A voice in my ear whispered 'Your wife is in the drosky—there is also an officer's cap and overcoat—the guards will let you pass—you can catch the Austrian express for Warsaw at Koluszki—the rest you can manage —all is paid for.' This hurried explanation took place close to where a drosky had halted. I jumped in, the driver started his three horses into their smartest pace, and, for the moment, I enjoyed freedom and happiness with wife and child. We bumped along the road merrily, and accepted with dignity the salute of the Cossack sentinel, who was too stupid to suspect anything wrong under my military disguise. He naturally supposed me to be a drunken officer indulging my thirst for pleasure. And so we escaped from Lodz, though it did seem hard to leave dozens of honest companions behind, who are now on the road to Siberia, simply because they could not arrange to bribe their jailers, as my wife did for me."

"But how did you manage the bribery?" I asked.

"Nothing simpler," answered he. "I can do anything in Poland, provided I have one or two rubles and one or two Jews. The Jews understand brokerage of every kind, and if you will take the trouble to study them and their ways, you soon discover them to be exceedingly useful under such a tyranny as the Russian. You or I, for instance, might have tried to bribe the jailer in such a blunt and clumsy manner as to have wasted not merely our money, but time as well. Or, what is worse, we might have given money in advance, and have had to pay double. In my case the Jew paid nothing until my body was delivered up at the drosky door, and then he paid only the market price, charging me the usual commission, perhaps 100 per cent."

"But how do you manage about crossing the frontier?" I asked.

"This is not quite so simple, yet less dangerous at this point than others. There is an extensive smuggling trade all along the western Russian border, one of the popular articles being tea from Königsberg, which is afterwards sold as caravan tea. Jews make the best smugglers, for obvious reasons; they will smuggle anything excepting revolutionary literature. Nowadays, a trade has sprung up that is very profitable—smuggling emigrants out of the country. This trade has assumed very large dimensions since the accession of Alexander III., and grows with every effort to Russify his subjects. It is safe to say that at least 100,000 have crossed the frontier at night during the last year, to say nothing of those who go by day with legitimate passes."

"But cannot every one get a pass?" I asked.

"They can, by paying for it; but it costs about 25 rubles, which is a great deal of money. To the peasant that represents two or three months' wages, at least. And even if he has that amount of money, the police do everything they can to prevent his leaving the country. They demand of him all sorts of certificates—of birth, baptism, residence, occupation, etc., which the most prudent man sometimes loses. Even if the poor devil has his certificates the police are sure to invent some charge upon which the peasant has to appear and pay a fine. In short, the innocent, along with the guilty, find it easier and cheaper to sneak across the border with the Jew smugglers, and run the risk of being shot, rather than attempt the journey in a legal manner. I suppose you have nothing of the kind in America, where every one is free?"

I had to admit that the Chinese entered the United States from British Columbia in very much the same manner, but that on the Pacific coast Chinese were supposed to have very wicked minds and no souls.

"But how do you make sure that the smugglers will not betray you to the frontier police?" I asked.

"Some do get cheated," he answered, "but that is because they are careless. When I came to Kovno I immediately made my agreement with a Jew, who promised to see me across the frontier, and for this I was to pay ten rubles. But I did not pay it to him—that would have been foolish. He took me to a rabbi, who is much respected here for his honesty, and to him I paid the money. The rabbi then gave me a token, a little bit of glass, which I keep on my person, and only give up to the smuggler after he has seen me safe over the line. Then I surrender my token to the smuggler, who receives the ten rubles from the rabbi on presentation of the token, and not before. In this way the whole transaction is consummated without any paper that might prove awkward in case of capture."

"But is it not wrong for a rabbi to lend himself to smuggling?"

"Who says anything about smuggling? I handed the rabbi ten rubles; he receipted for it by handing me a piece of glass; he pays the ten rubles out again to any one who brings him this identical bit of glass! There is nothing illegal in that. All the police of Russia would fail to hold him on such a charge. But, besides, you must remember that you are in a country where no trade of any kind can be transacted without lying and bribing; the government leads the way in rascality of every kind, and if you expect the Jews to be outwitted by Russian police, you will be much mistaken.

Our little steamer had been winding in and out among shallows, dodging the great rafts that come down from the Minsk forests, and we were nearing the frontier. The steamer suddenly turned towards the bank.

"Good-bye!" said my friend; "perhaps I shall meet you in America. Two smugglers are to slip off here; I go with them; we shall make for the woods and take our chances when it is dark —good-bye!"

The steamer closed well with the right bank, so that the counter extended over the land. A long boat-hook was planted in the mud; my friend seized it; one, two, three were counted, and with the help of the steamer's mate he was pushed off towards the shore, landing safely. The two Jews followed, using the big boat-hook as a vaulting-pole. The last Jew fell on his back in the mud; their bags and bundles were tumbled after them, the wheels revolved once more, and in a few moments the three lonely figures were out of sight. I asked the captain why he dropped passengers at that point.

"Oh, it is near to their village!" I thought he winked as he said this, but am not quite sure.

Later on, that evening, Remington and I were ploughing through the deep sandy track that runs from Jurburg to the Prussian frontier. The distance was about six miles—all of it through a wilderness of pine forest, in which the only creatures we passed was a squadron of cavalry quartered in a long, straggling row of peasant huts. Our driver was a venerable Jew, in a long gabardine, curly hair falling upon his shoulders, a silk cap, a curl in front of each ear, a pair of topboots.

"Smuggling," said he, "is the only business at which we can earn a living. The people live by it, and it helps pay the salaries of the police. We sometimes get shot, but one must do something for a living. The Russian government compels all the Jews to live only in a small part of Russia. The struggle for life is terrible here —so terrible that plenty of men spend theirs carrying loads in and out of Prussia."

"Are there many soldiers on the frontier?" I asked.

"They are so thick," he said, "that I wonder they do not shoot one another by mistake. Every thousand feet brings you to a picket close to the line; then two miles behind that is a cordon made of two foot-soldiers to every one cavalryman, and eight miles back of the frontier is a complete line of Cossack or dragoon cavalry; so you see, even if the first line is evaded, there are two more left to catch you."

Suddenly, in the midst of the forest, we came upon a log-hut, in front of which were two high posts. The road, or sand-trail, was here barred by a heavy chain, and a soldier mounted guard by its side. Remington and I were ordered to stop, enter the hut, have our baggage searched, and our passports scrutinized. As this occupied an hour, I had ample time to note that every passenger arriving from Prussia not merely had his baggage searched, but his very person examined; under his armpits, down his back, to his very skin. I had seen Chinamen treated in this brutal manner on landing in San Francisco before the passing of the Exclusion Bill, but I had not expected to find it elsewhere, not even in Russia. As Remington and I were travelling on "special" passports, signed by the secretary of state, and as Russia had just received four cargoes of wheat as a present from our country to her starving people, we had looked forward to some consideration at the hands of the officials; but, so far as I could gather, they had never heard of America or our cargoes; the censor, perhaps, regarded both as suspicious. One of the customs officials spoke bad German and meant to be polite; the chief, however, had the features of a Persian, was disfigured by scrofula, and had the amiability of an Apache. The only sign of happiness he gave was when the report of a rifle came through the woods.

"Another Jew," he said, and grinned the grin of a mean-spirited brute who knew that when a smuggler was shot part of his pack fell to the share of the customs official.

That shot struck my Polish friend—nothing but a flesh wound, however. The two Jews helped him on, he was close to the frontier, and three days afterwards I shook hands with him at Königsberg, on his way to Hamburg. He was beaming with happiness, his wife and child were with him, his arm was in a sling, but doing well. He was sustained by the thought that at last he was beyond the reach of a Russian policeman, and would soon be in a country where Russification was unknown.

Shortly after the Polish insurrection of 1830, in which the German provinces had no share, the Czar Nicholas concluded to Russify on a large scale, and sent, therefore, as chief of the whole educational system of the Baltic provinces, an illiterate Russian general. He began with the university at Dorpat,* the model university of the country, and ordered (1835) that henceforth professors and students should appear only in military uniform. Dorpat was founded in the same year as Yale, and has been conducted to this day in the same enlightened spirit. Imagine President Dwight, at New Haven, receiving from the New York Board of Aldermen an order to appear henceforth only in the regalia of St. Patrick; it could not produce a greater sensation than was produced when this great German seat of learning was handed over into the coarse hands of a professional soldier for prompt Russification. Henceforth the Russian language was obligatory, and the appointment of professors rested no longer with the faculty, but with the military director.

So much for the cause of popular education.

---

* Since writing this the very name Dorpat has been suppressed, and a Russian one ordered in its stead.

The seed planted by that Russian general has been nursed and watered by others equally hostile to German culture, and the laws passed in the last few years should surprise no one familiar with the spirit of laws passed during the last fifty or one hundred years.

The religious Russification has a history almost as painful as that of Dorpat University and the schools, but want of space forbids my entering on it here. The whole country is Protestant from time immemorial, and jogged along very happily with its Lutheran clergymen, who felt secure from orthodox intrigue because they trusted the promises of successive czars. One fine day in 1836, however, news came that Riga, the chief commercial town of the Baltic provinces, was to have an orthodox bishop, and that a seminary for Greek priests was also to be erected near by. To be sure, there were scarcely any orthodox worshippers, but the priests were confident that, with the police and the name of the czar behind them, they would soon make the Lutherans feel their power—and they did.

The year 1841 came. There had been three years of very bad harvest; the peasants in remote villages were in a desperate condition; there was much discontent on all sides, and, as is usual in such a state of things, the fault is always laid at the door of the landlord, or the employer of labor. When things were at their worst, the Greek priests sent crafty emissaries throughout the distressed regions, much as the Jesuits do in China. These told the ignorant peasants that the czar had millions of acres of rich land in the warm South for all those who were loyal to him, and believed as he believed. Pretty soon peasants commenced to appear in the town, applying to the authorities for free farms in the promised land of sunshine and deep soil. But the secular authorities knew nothing of the trick by which the Greek priests had lured them from their country, and, of course, told them they had been fooled, and must go home. The poor people had, in many cases, sold everything in order to make the journey, and felt desperate when told they had been duped. As they turned away from the town-hall, however, they were steered by a priestly decoy to the orthodox quarter; the promise of land was repeated—all they were to do was to be baptized in the faith of the czar. The priest told them how wicked it was to have a different religion from that of the emperor, and that all those who held the orthodox faith had rather a good time in this world, and a sure thing in the world to come.

Now all such propaganda would in ordinary times have been wasted, but after three years of hard times, and with minds unsettled by promises of fertile lands, the orthodox priests had an opportunity of the most exceptional kind. The argument which, however, swept away their conscientious doubts most completely was that the czar personally desired them all to become of his religion, and that to be unorthodox was to be disloyal to their ruler. There were few Lithuanian peasants who could resist such an appeal to their patriotism, for to such a one the czar's wish is law. To explain the conversions that became very numerous in the next few years, it must also be understood that, whereas the orthodox priests moved about with the insolent assurance of representing the czar and his police, the Lutheran clergy had no prestige beyond the province from which they drew their congregation and meagre pay. By the law of Russia they were not an independent power—merely a tolerated sect. The large mass of Lithuanian peasants were Lutheran from habit; few of them understood the grounds of their belief, as does the average New-Englander. Among these simple people went orthodox agents, who gave them the assurance that the Lutheran worship was substantially the same as the Greek, and that in changing they were only drawing nearer to their great father, the czar. And, indeed, during the early period of the orthodox propaganda, say from 1836 to 1846, the Greek priests allowed their converts from Protestantism to retain their Lutheran hymns, even to retain the reading of a sermon; but this was done only as a decoy for the others. The peasants went among their hesitating neighbors saying that they had lost none of their old worship, but, on the contrary, had now a much easier time of it.

The reader exclaims: " But why did not the Lutherans preach against the orthodox heresy?" They tried to, but their mouths were stopped by the orthodox police. Clergymen who dared criticise the Greek church, or even to enlighten their people upon the distinction between Protestantism and orthodoxy, were sent to jail. The Lutheran Church had its catechism suppressed by the police. Wherever the Lutheran Church came in conflict with the orthodox interests, the Russian police saw to it that the czar's cause did not suffer. The czar had the censor on his side, so that while his coreligionists might say what they chose against the religion of Luther, it was made a crime to make a defence against these attacks.

The peasants found that the promises of rich lands were not kept, and that the orthodox priests were as greedy for money as other men. Many wanted to get back into their old Church, but it was too late. They had forfeited the right to think for themselves; they were flogged if they attended a Lutheran worship, and it was a criminal act for a Lutheran clergyman to allow one of his former flock to return to him—to even let him attend service. If one of these newly-fledged orthodox peasantry married, the czar's Church claimed all the children, even though the mother were Protestant, and though the father desired his children to become Lutheran.

The little picture I have given is matter of history—it would seem to belong to the sixteenth century—yet it is a perfect reflection of what is going on to-day in the most civilized portion of the czar's dominion.

The *censorship* has played an important part in the Russification of these provinces—even more injurious a part than in Russia. Shortly after the French Revolution the czar determined to stamp out all independent thinking, and commenced his work in the Baltic provinces by suppressing a volume of Protestant sermons by M. Sontagg, a preacher who corresponded in Riga to Spurgeon in London or Beecher in America. Another clergyman was condemned to be flogged, and to hard labor in the penitentiary, because in his library were found the works of Lafontaine. In 1800 all books, without exception, were shut out from the Baltic provinces, on the ground that there were already enough for practical purposes. It was a hard law on those who had ordered books and paid in advance, but no exception was made. Fortunately, it lasted only four years, when the censor once more appeared, and with it comparative liberty. To give one an idea of how much is meant by this, it need only be said that, under Nicholas, no paper was allowed to discuss foreign affairs; the utmost allowed was to copy what had already appeared in the government gazette. No paper could mention any item of news about the court without first obtaining permission of the czar's chief palace servant; no news of any kind could appear without first being submitted to the chief of the department whom it might affect directly or indirectly. If a ship was wrecked the ministry of marine must be consulted; if a pocket was picked, the police; damage to crops comes within the province of the agricultural department; when a military review takes place, nothing must be said until the secretary of war has been consulted. The censor is not materially different to-day, let us add in parenthesis. Here is an illustration:

A distinguished political writer, the editor of the leading newspaper in western Russia, lately wrote an article (August, 1892) criticising Bismarck for his obstructionistic attitude towards the German emperor and Caprivi. The writer is a man whose word I respect, and he told me the story at my own table, immediately on arrival across the Russian border.

When he learned that his article had been suppressed he was very indignant, and therefore called upon the president of the "censure," whom he knew very well, and who had always treated him with great consideration, owing to his high social and literary position. The conversation was about as follows:

*Author:* "I know that I have no right to ask your excellency about a suppressed work, but if your excellency would be so good as to make an exception in my case—"
*Censor:* "But, my dear friend, why in the world should you to-day write an article against Bismarck?"
*Author:* "Because, your excellency, I am a Monarchist, and Bismarck seeks to undermine the influence of a monarch!"
*Censor:* "It never struck me from that standpoint. But why do you not show your love for monarchy by studying our gracious majesty, the czar?"
*Author:* "Because, as your excellency is aware, the police forbid my writing anything whatsoever about the czar. I may only copy the Court Circular."
*Censor:* "H'm, true, I did not think of that. But you cannot print the article against Bismarck."
*Author:* "But would not your excellency kindly hint the reason, so that in future my pen may conform more fully with your excellency's views?"
*Censor:* "No, I should not; but still, as an old friend, you may as well know: the government regards your criticism of Bismarck as an indirect approval of the German emperor. Now, you must know that his majesty the czar does not desire to have the German emperor praised, directly or indirectly. Good-morning!"

My friend returns to Russia in a few days, and as I do not wish to hear of his being sent to jail or Siberia, I am forced to keep to myself many details that would put the police on his track. It is sufficiently illustrative of Russian journalism, however, to know that nothing can come to print about the German emperor that does not abuse him personally, or at least praise his enemies.

Not long since, on the occasion of dedicating a Protestant church in the Baltic provinces, the clergyman, thinking thereby to emphasize the tolerance of the community, as well as the friendly ties uniting all sections, used these words:

"It is an elevating thought that, not merely Protestants, but orthodox and Jews, have helped us in the building of this edifice, by giving us money contributions."

The censor regarded this sentiment as an insult to the czar's coreligionists, and suppressed the report of the affair in the Dorpat newspaper. On another occasion, a statistical table had been prepared with great care, discussing the future careers of students in the Baltic schools according to nationalities. The censor suppressed it because Russians appeared unfavorably as compared with those of German extraction. This is as comical as though the negroes of Louisiana caused the suppression of our decennial census because the whites of Massachusetts appeared to advantage.

Imagine now the happiness of the theatre-manager who makes himself responsible for the rent of the building and the wages of his players. He dares not risk much in the purchase of a new play, for before it can be produced it must be sent to St. Petersburg for approval, and after it is performed it is still subject to be suppressed at any moment if a costume, a gesture, an inflection, a local hit, or any trifle should, in the mind of the local police, be calculated to produce unfavorable comparison between the government of the czar and that of any one else. Out of two hundred plays sent by one theatre-director alone, in Mitau, scarcely twenty came back with the requisite license, and it took many months to accomplish even this much. Did the Russian police act in this manner because they consider theatres a means of improper recreation? Not in the least. The Russian police encourage licentiousness to any extent, from dram-shops to houses of ill-fame. They seek their friends in the conquered countries, not among the respectable and constructive elements of society, but among the dissolute and degraded. The censorship they exercise is not to keep from publicity impure sentiments or indecent suggestions; these are to be found in every resort of Russian officials. What the censor does not allow, however, is any public expression that savors of reasoning. One play is forbidden because it suggests nationality; another because it suggests patriotism—both obviously inflammatory concepts in the minds of oppressed people. A play referring favorably either to the Protestant or Catholic clergy cannot be tolerated because it suggests comparison with that of the czar. No play can be produced calculated to weaken respect for the monarch, his ministers, his police, or his officials; in fact, we can hardly imagine a modern farce which the Russian censor would not be able to construe as dangerous to the peace of what he is pleased to regard as society. There is hardly a play of Shakespeare that could be played in Riga to-day, to say nothing of the comedies that sparkle at theatres like Daly's in New York. Every night, in every theatre of the Baltic provinces, there sits a government spy to report if anything is done, either on or off the stage, calculated to strengthen German or weaken Russian influence. Under these circumstances, is it likely that dramatic art should flourish? Yet, on the Baltic, as in Poland, the people have ceased protesting on this point—they have begun to anticipate the time when their very mother-tongue will be forbidden, not only in the school, but in the pulpit and on the stage.

The aggravating feature of Russian censorship is not merely that the censors are, as a rule, grossly illiterate people, but that the honestly patriotic writer is never protected against caprice. For instance, one article discussed the life of the agitator Alexander Herzen, considered him a bad man, an enthusiast, but still considered that he was *honest*. For allowing him this one attribute the police of St. Petersburg were indignant. Another paper in its columns stated that the Roman revolution progressed *bravely*. Down came the censor, and remarked that bravery in connection with any revolution was ridiculous and inflammatory. In the university town of Dorpat the censor forbade the publication of the programme of the Communists of Paris in 1848, although the censors in St. Petersburg had passed it there. The reason was that, while good Russians might hear such news, it might prove inflammatory in a province of persecuted Germans.

A Jewish pawnbroker advertised a sale — among other things of a *church* organ. Censor struck out the word *church*, substituting instead the word *large*. Reason given was that the presence of a church organ at a Jew sale was calculated to undermine respect for religion. Another paper in Mitau announced the arrival of the governor-general in the same list with those of other notable arrivals. Censor struck the name out, on the ground that it was calculated to decrease the dignity of the czar's government if a high official's name appeared along with that of ordinary people.

An article on France declared the word *Jacquerie* as meaning a species of peasant rebellion. The censor struck the whole passage out as being superfluous — as suggesting disorder.

Another paper stated that crabs turned red when boiled, turning red with shame at having gone backward so much. The censor struck this out, for to every German reader the crab could only refer to the government of the Russian czar! An interesting admission under any circumstances.

Police censorship is much stricter to-day than it was when Prussia and Russia joined hands in hunting down what they were jointly pleased to consider political heresy. In the early part of this century Prussian official newspapers were regarded in Russia as quite fit for perusal, even by people in the Baltic provinces. To-day, however, the literature of Germany is regarded as more deadly to Russian peace than even that of republican France, to say nothing of England and America.

The memorandum-book of a censor, now dead, came curiously to light on our side of the frontier a short time since. He appears to have been an honest man, and in his dying moments so pricked by a sense of his past wickedness that by way of smoothing his path into eternity he resolved to expose some of the deviltry of which he was made a tool. One fine day he was sent, in company with a police colonel from St. Petersburg to Riga, with orders to inspect every library, and see that nothing dangerous was being read in this commercial centre of the Baltic provinces. Riga is a seaport town with 175,000 intelligent and industrious people. It has a famous polytechnic or scientific school, three colleges, and many schools and learned societies. This fact made it appear the more dangerous to the "Third Section" in St. Petersburg, and it was determined to suddenly search the town, just as the rooms of students and editors are periodically broken into in Moscow or Odessa. The police mission was, of course, kept a secret, and the governor at Riga was ordered to put all the local police agencies into action, in order that as much should be discovered as possible. A raid was made at the same time upon the university town of Dorpat, the centre of intellectual activity not only in the Baltic provinces but of all Russia. Its library has 200,000 volumes, its faculties have compared favorably with those of Heidelberg or Göttingen, its astronomical observatory is one of the best in the world. If any spot might be regarded as deserving fair treatment, even in Russia, Dorpat surely was, for its constitution had been repeatedly guaranteed by the solemn promises of successive czars since Peter the Great.

But the fanatical zeal for Russification would not be limited by mere promises, and so it happened that, one night in July, at exactly eleven o'clock, the censor and police agent arrived, and immediately placed their seal upon the doors of

the three chief booksellers, as well as those of
the leading circulating library. The book-dealers
not only had to have their places closed while
each title-page was being scrutinized and compared with the list of permitted or forbidden
books, but they had to furnish the police with
their cash-books and ledgers, to tell what books
they had sold, what were ordered, and *for whom*.
It turned out, in the course of a fortnight, that
over one thousand books were regarded as either
forbidden, suspected, or unknown to the czar's
censors. But, worse than that, about a hundred
forbidden books had been sold. The police now
ransacked every private house to get these back;
the booksellers had to pay a heavy fine, and the
confiscated books were carted to St. Petersburg
to the library of the " Third Section." Remembering that Dorpat is a quiet little seat of learning, with a population of barely 30,000, we may
imagine the indignation caused by closing every
book-shop for two weeks, and having the houses
of men of letters ransacked by policemen. And
what were the books which the czar regarded as
poisonous to the orthodox mind? Among them
we find those of Louis Blanc, Proudhon, Lamartine, Heine, and, as the wickedest of all, Thiers's
famous history of the Napoleonic era, *The Consulate and Empire*. Imagine the pleasure of
literary life in a country where it is a crime to
read such books. It is needless to say that the

police hunted particularly for every book that did not speak well of Russian government.

On the 9th of July the literary inquisition was opened in Riga. There were 200,000 volumes to inspect, 2300 business letters to read, and 5500 invoices to compare. From the 9th to the 20th the police occupied every book-shop in the Baltic capital, and finally carted off to St. Petersburg 2042 confiscated works—among these 619 not exactly forbidden, but simply confiscated because the local censor knew nothing about them, and therefore presumed them to be heretical. Oddly enough, many of the books confiscated had been bought under orders for Russian seats of learning in the interior, Kieff University among others. The St. Petersburg police were furious at hearing that 2000 dangerous books had been found in Riga, and secured from the czar an order to close every book-shop in the town. This meant bankruptcy. The blockade lasted four months—only on Christmas Eve did the czar suspend his judgment, too late, however, for the sellers to profit by the general Christmas trade. In suspending the measure, however, he ordered the arrest of every bookseller, pending a police investigation, which lasted two years and one month, after which they were all set at liberty upon paying a handsome fine.

Does not one's blood boil at reading of such disgraceful government—all done in the name of

Russification? Think of the hundreds of schoolchildren who cannot buy the books for their classes; the professional men who find themselves incapable of receiving the latest contribution in their particular department. The Chinese emperor who built the Great Wall destroyed all the books he could find in order that future ages might regard him as the first man in history. Russian monarchs act in an even more drastic manner—they do not only suppress the books that have been, but take equal pains that their own generation shall produce none worth reading.

And what were these 2000 books confiscated at Riga? Among them were 131 copies of Thiers's *History of the Consulate and Empire*, and 94 Thiers's *History of the Revolution*. There were 91 volumes of Lamartine's *History of the Girondists*, and 652 parts of a popular encyclopædia. Here alone are 1000 out of the 2004 accounted for—all confiscated as being dangerous to the czar's government—yet books deemed suitable for the library of a civilized student in any other part of the world.

Had the censor and his policemen confined themselves to legal procedure the outrage upon decency would have been great, but in the instance I cite even the Russian governor-general protested to the czar that every form of law was trampled underfoot, that honest and leading citizens were condemned and punished without a trial, and that their private papers were ransacked by the police without the slightest legal warrant. His protest accomplished nothing, unless we regard as clemency two years' arrest, a fine, and a four months' closing of shop.

And all this took place, and is daily repeating itself, in a land living under the most solemn guarantees from successive Russian monarchs!

The key-note is " Russification " in school, Church, university, and public service. The year before France and Germany went to war, or, to be accurate, on the 15th of October, 1869, the adjutant of Alexander II., General Albedinsky, formulated a programme for checking the Protestant and German aspirations of these provinces—concluding with the advice that the czar should not be bound by the pledges of his ancestors, but—"That the Baltic provinces should be melted into the Russian empire unconditionally and irrevocably." This has been Russian policy here as in Poland, and it has been growing in severity and brutality during the years that Bismarck sought to make his people and his emperor believe that Russia was a good friend to Germany and German civilization. The cries of persecuted Germans found no echo in the heart of the Iron Chancellor—he was persecuting his own enemies so hotly that he had no time to attend to the sufferings of those beyond his frontier.

Bismarck, happily for his country, is no longer the German government, and there are signs in the political firmament indicating that the Germany of to-day will not remain much longer silent while fellow-creatures of kindred blood, language, and faith are crying desperately for help, only a few miles from their eastern towns. The German emperor has already notified his neighbors that humanity has upon him claims quite as sacred as those of statecraft, and every man who loves liberty must surely long for the moment when he shall demand an explanation in St. Petersburg of the long series of diabolical acts of official cruelty perpetrated in the name of "Russification."

THE END

www.ingramcontent.com/pod-product-compliance
Lightning Source LLC
Chambersburg PA
CBHW020248240426
43672CB00006B/663